"Early in the book, Charles Phua quoted Humpty Dumpty: when I use a word, it means just what I choose it to mean – neither more nor less. Pragmatism is perhaps one such word. By discussing pragmatism in the context of how three very different countries view it – China, the United States and Singapore – Phua has been able to develop a conceptual framework for the analysis of the word in academic discourse and distinguish between its use in social conversation and as an organising principle in statecraft."

– **George Yeo**, *former Foreign Minister, Republic of Singapore*

"Dr Charles Phua has written a book that uniquely considers how the philosophy of pragmatism, in both practice and principles, influences the exercise of foreign policy and statecraft in nations. In particular, he carefully examines the policies and approaches of China, the United States and Singapore, and considers how each nation is shaped by a blend of idealism, realism and contextual opportunities and constraints. As we move towards a more complex geopolitical environment, Dr Phua's book offers fascinating ideas on how nations mould their agendas and fashion their policy formulations and implementations."

– **Professor Tan Eng Chye**, *President, National University of Singapore*

"As the world changes, foreign policy must change. As this book makes clear, pragmatic foreign policy is needed to contend not just with politics narrowly understood but also with the full range of global challenges: economic, social, climate and others."

– **Professor Craig Calhoun**, *University Professor of Social Sciences, Arizona State University, former President of the London of School of Economics and Social Sciences Research Council (SSRC)*

"A highly original and interesting book that compares and connects Chinese, Singaporean and American thinking on foreign policy. There is much food for thought for scholars and practitioners to ponder."

– **Professor Qin Yaqing**, *former President, Chinese Foreign Affairs University*

"Is Singapore's foreign policy based on realism, as many have claimed? Dr Phua is right to say it is not. It is based on pragmatism or a combination of realism and idealism in pragmatism."

– **Professor Tommy Koh**, *Ambassador-at-Large, Ministry of Foreign Affairs, Singapore, and former President, Third United Nations Conference on the Law of the Sea*

"A well-analysed book on pragmatism in foreign policy, a topic that has not received much attention in scholarly debates. The case studies are illuminating."

– **T.V. Paul**, *James McGill Professor of International Relations, McGill University, Canada, former President, International Studies Association, and author of Restraining Great Powers: Soft Balancing from Empires to the Global Era (Yale University Press, 2018)*

"'Pragmatism' is a slippery term, touching on different domains of human behaviour – psychological, philosophical, social, political, economic and others. Charles Chao Rong Phua's book takes an interdisciplinary approach to case

studies – China, Singapore, the United States – in order to delineate the "system[s] that supports 'being pragmatic'" and thus provides the context for pragmatism in the contemporary global order."
– **Professor Robbie Goh**, *Provost, Singapore University of Social Sciences*

"It is hard to do justice to the scholarly range of this challenging book which ranges from the mysteries of Daoism to the emerging properties of American decision-making. The author rightly warns that we need strategic pragmatism more than ever – perhaps it is timely to recalibrate the pendulum swings between 'strategic narcissism' and 'strategic autism' tendencies, both of which are threatening world peace."
– **Professor Christopher Coker**, *Director, LSE IDEAS*

"Pragmatism has long been held up as a primary organising concept for policy-making. But what does pragmatism mean in the policy context? And how are we to understand its application in the process of policy formulation? By way of a comparative study of the United States, China and Singapore, Charles Phua helps us navigate these complex conceptual and practical issues. This book should be essential reading for those interested in the fundamental philosophical underpinnings of 'pragmatic' policy thinking and making."
– **Professor Joseph Chinyong Liow**, *Dean of Humanities, Arts and Social Sciences, Nanyang Technological University*

"This is an intriguing and systematic assessment of pragmatism as an element of foreign policy formulation and implementation in three very different states. The author draws out some important practical implications for policymakers from his study, and one can only agree with his concluding argument that future generations would benefit from pragmatic responses to complex global challenges such as managing climate change and ensuring environmental sustainability."
– **Dr Tim Huxley**, *former Executive Director, IISS-Asia*

"A must-read for anyone seeking to understand how China's 'idiosyncratic mixture of principle and pragmatism' shapes its relations with the rest of the world."
– **Professor Carla P. Freeman**, *Executive Director, SAIS Foreign Policy Institute, Johns Hopkins University*

"A solid contribution to the study of what the author calls strategic pragmatism in foreign policy, with the fascinating comparative illustrations of the United States, China and Singapore. Insightful and thought-provoking, while necessarily controversial in some points of the policies conducted by the three states."
– **Professor Shi Yinhong**, *Distinguished Professor of International Relations, Renmin University of China*

"Charles has written a creative piece linking philosophy, public policy and international affairs. It is worth a read to examine its implications to our theory and practice of international affairs in both the United States and China."
– **Professor Wang Yizhou**, *Boya Chair Professor and Associate Dean, School of International Studies, Peking University*

"By operationalising pragmatism, a frequently used but vague and elusive term, Phua not only successfully develops a conceptual framework of foreign policy but also succinctly substantiates it by the foreign policy practice of China, the United States and Singapore in a way that will be useful to academics and practitioners alike. An original work on pragmatic foreign policy!"

— **Professor Zhang Qingmin**, *Chair, Department of Diplomacy, School of International Studies, Peking University*

"This book seeks to be a synthetic primer on Pragmatism as applied in US, Chinese and Singaporean foreign policies. Moreover, Pragmatisms in the three countries are subtly different. This book not only helps us to understand current policies of the three countries, but it also constructs a theoretical framework of Pragmatism for foreign international politics in the world."

— **Professor Xufeng Zhu**, *Associate Dean, School of Public Policy and Management, Tsinghua University*

"Towards Strategic Pragmatism in Foreign Policy crafts a unique and integrative approach, embodying both academic rigor and practical relevance in treating the role of pragmatism in political process. Charles Chao Rong Phua unfolds a paradigm for optimising unstable equilibria amidst ever-shifting currents of public policy, national interest, international relations and geostrategic positioning. He authoritatively reconciles variegated meanings and nuances of pragmatism, without contradiction, among three contrasting polities: China, the United States and Singapore. This original and illuminating work is highly recommended!"

— **Lou Marinoff**, *PhD. Professor of Philosophy and Asian Studies, The City College of New York, founding President of the American Philosophical Practitioners Association and author of The Middle Way*

"Charles Chao Rong Phua offers an important corrective to the realist notion that international structure compels pragmatism in foreign policy. Through a close examination of Chinese, American and Singapore foreign policies, Phua establishes that pragmatic leaders necessarily act as realists simultaneously in both domestic politics and international politics and that pragmatism is filtered through leadership personalities. Foreign policy pragmatism may be the ideal of realists, but it is illusive, except in the extreme. More generally, Phua shows that foreign policy tends toward a hybrid mix of the imperatives of personal politics and international politics."

— **Professor Robert S. Ross**, *Professor of Political Science at Boston College and Associate, John King Fairbank Center for Chinese Studies, Harvard University*

Towards Strategic Pragmatism in Foreign Policy

What is pragmatism? Is it a means to an end, or an end in itself? Is it antithetical to ideology or morality?

Arguing that pragmatism is a skill much more than an attribute, Phua examines how viewing it in this way can help achieve better foreign policy outcomes. He examines and contrasts the ways in which the United States, China and Singapore have incorporated pragmatism into their approaches to foreign policy. In doing so, he debunks dualistic myths around pragmatism and ideology and promotes the view of pragmatism as a skill that can be developed.

An essential primer for students, analysts and policymakers, with a fresh and practical approach to pragmatism.

Charles Chao Rong Phua runs Solaris Strategies Singapore (and Solaris Consortium of Management Consultancies) dedicated to pragmatically solving complex problems supporting governments, corporates and underserved non-profits at sector and enterprise levels, after two decades in government, where he functioned as head research trainer in defence and chief external affairs supporting cities and infrastructural diplomacy. Charles also presides over the Association for Public Affairs (Singapore), spearheading active citizenry in policy-making and served as chief judge for Singapore Model Cabinet and Parliament organised by the government.

He is an internationally certified management consultant and agile certified practitioner with a doctorate in public policy, degrees in international relations, security management, education, accounting, and completed executive education in strategy, innovation, entrepreneurship, sustainability, marketing from leading business schools: Harvard, MIT, Stanford, Wharton, Kellogg, Berkeley, Babson, INSEAD, Cambridge, Oxford, London Business School.

He currently serves as the series editor for Routledge series for strategy, wisdom and skills with a commitment to codify practitioner + academic wisdom in applied and interdisciplinary fields.

Routledge-Solaris Focus on Strategy, Wisdom and Skill

The Series is advised and edited by Charles Chao Rong Phua, the Chairman of the Solaris Consortium of Management Consultancies.

Towards Strategic Pragmatism in Foreign Policy
Cases of United States of America, China and Singapore
Charles Chao Rong Phua

Towards Strategic Pragmatism in Foreign Policy

Cases of United States of America, China and Singapore

Charles Chao Rong Phua

Routledge
Taylor & Francis Group

LONDON AND NEW YORK

First published 2022
by Routledge
2 Park Square, Milton Park, Abingdon, Oxon OX14 4RN

and by Routledge
605 Third Avenue, New York, NY 10158

Routledge is an imprint of the Taylor & Francis Group, an Informa business

© 2022 Charles Chao Rong Phua

British Library Cataloguing-in-Publication Data
A catalogue record for this book is available from the British Library

Library of Congress Cataloging-in-Publication Data
A catalog record has been requested for this book

ISBN: 978-1-032-06540-3 (hbk)
ISBN: 978-1-032-06541-0 (pbk)
ISBN: 978-1-003-20272-1 (ebk)

DOI: 10.4324/9781003202721

Typeset in Galliard
by Apex CoVantage, LLC

MIX
Paper from
responsible sources
FSC
www.fsc.org   FSC™ C013985

Printed in the United Kingdom
by Henry Ling Limited

Contents

Foreword   xi
List of tables   xiii
List of acronyms   xiv

1 A pragmatic definition of pragmatism:
   problem-solving approach   1

PART I
What is pragmatism?   7

2 Fitness beats truth: towards a definition of pragmatism   9

3 Big-P and Small-P pragmatism, strategic
   pragmatism and grand strategy   14

4 Agential and structural factors of (pragmatic)
   production   18

5 Pragmatism in policy process framework   21

6 Varieties of pragmatism   27

PART II
China   35

7 The dao of pragmatism: going with the flow
   without being swept away   37

8 Seeking truth from facts   43

9 Red lines (and pink lines) in Chinese foreign policy   49

PART III
Singapore   57

10 The ideology of pragmatism   59

11 A friend to everybody and an ally to none   66

12 The geography of pragmatism   77

PART IV
The United States   85

13 The system (systemic pendulums) of pragmatism   87

14 Small-P and Big-P pragmatism on the election trail   95

15 How the emergent properties of the US system
     force unpragmatic actors to make pragmatic decisions   102

PART V
What have we Learnt?   107

16 Varieties of pragmatism: muddling through, in style   109

17 Strategic and systemic pragmatism through
     dynamic equilibria . . .   119

Bibliography   122
Interviews   143
Questionnaires   147
Index   151

Foreword

Pragmatism, if it is deemed a positive word, then every politician will say this is a 'pragmatic' policy. The converse is true. After a while, what does Pragmatism really mean becomes lost . . . Unfortunately, we could probably substitute Pragmatism with fads like 'liberal', 'sustainability', and this truism probably still rings true.

The meaning of a word is socially constructed, however objective the research or researcher claims to be. Is social construction or culturally subjective necessarily inferior in the face of the purported high altar of Enlightenment objectivity? Certainly, no. I would venture to posit that this subjectivity and cultural diversity are precisely what makes us humans and the inquiry of human affairs interesting and ever dynamic. Every culture may have a different perspective on a particular word or concept and may in fact operationalise it in different ways. Merely examining cultural perspectives of any concept constitutes a worthy Lakatosian research programme.

This book is a start of a Pragmatism Lakatosian research programme which I am committing my entire professional life to discover and grow as both a practitioner (running a trisector consultancy consortium: Solaris Strategies Singapore serving governments, corporates and underserved non-profits) and academic (adjunct faculty specialising in strategy-innovation problem-solving practicums and series editor for Routledge-Solaris series on strategy, wisdom and skills). Pragmatism intrigues me because it relates to problem solving/practical reason (Aristotelian phronesis) in a sea of theories (Aristotelian episteme/universal truth) where every theory seems correct, to an extent but none are wiser. However, when I dive deeper, there is the philosophical pragmatism (which started as a distinctive New World America's school of thought versus Old Europe/Continental philosophy, but unfortunately lost shine to the bulk of 20th century until Richard Rorty sought to revive it), political, policy pragmatism variants; Chinese used pragmatism as almost a way of life. Everyone seems to be saying something on pragmatism but there is no coherent conceptual framework that synthesises the inherent relationship in a clear manner.

This book seeks to be a synthetic primer on Pragmatism as applied in foreign policy, using the US, China and Singapore cases. Foreign policy is deliberately chosen over public policy for the inherent challenge to bridge international–national levels of analysis. Foreign policy is often an extension of domestic policy and is formulated from a national decision-making apparatus. Unfortunately, not all public policy theorists are familiar with international relations, and converse is true. But I happen to be trained in both disciplines as an academic and practitioner, hence I sought to bridge these two inherently inter-disciplinary fields in this primer. Also, this primer seeks to marry both disciplinary (public policy and international relations) and area studies (the US, China and Singapore) approaches. The key argument is that being pragmatic is not a permanent attribute, but a characteristic moment by moment, decision by decision, action by action. Being pragmatic does not equate to success but being unpragmatic will likely lead to failure. More successful countries have a policy choice to be unpragmatic but risk negative repercussions. I hope readers pardon any shortcomings or shortfalls in expectations in this fairly ambitious primer.

Nonetheless, I hope this is a start for like-minded scholars to apply the Pragmatism framework to other cases to refine it and enhance its external validity. I hope to seek the help of like-minded community of scholar–practitioner–comrades to grow this 'Towards Strategic Pragmatism in Foreign Policy' in an agile manner. My next step is to explore the nexus between strategy and pragmatism, in both public policy and business disciplines.

Charles Chao Rong Phua
Singapore

Tables

3.1   The pragmatism continuum   15
5.1   Four Theories of foreign policy (Gideon Rose)   22
16.1 The pragmatism continuum   114

Acronyms

ABC	All But Clinton
ASEAN	Association of Southeast Asian Nations
CCI	China-Singapore Connectivity Initiative
CCP	Chinese Communist Party
EDB	Economic Development Board (Singapore)
EU	European Union
FOSS	Forum of Small States
G7	Group of 7
G20	Group of 20
HAIR	Helicopter, Analysis, Imagination, Reality
HQ	headquarters
IR	International Relations
KMT	Kuomintang
KTM	Keretapi Tanah Melayu
MCP	Malayan Communist Party
MITI	Ministry of Trade and Industry (Japan)
OBOR	One Belt One Road
PRC	People's Republic of China
SALT	Strategic Arms Limitation Treaty
SIP	Singapore-China Suzhou Industrial Park
STC	Southern Transport Corridor
START	Strategic Arms Reduction Treaty
TECP	Tianjin Eco-City Project
UK	United Kingdom
UN	United Nations
UNTAC	United Nations Transitional Authority of Cambodia
US	United States
USSR	Union of Soviet Socialist Republics

1 A pragmatic definition of pragmatism

Problem-solving approach

The concept of pragmatism, in a truly pragmatic fashion, lends itself to multiple interpretations. It tends to be a "you know it when you see it" thing. Thus, for example, most people would recognise Deng Xiaoping's famous statement that "it does not matter whether a cat is black or white, if it catches mice it is a good cat", as being pragmatic. However, there is a fine line between pragmatism and hypocrisy, and before studying one it is important to distinguish it from the other. So how can this be done?

The lazy answer – and one that has been given by many in the past – would be "means and ends". A hypocrite is willing to fight for any cause, while a pragmatist is willing to accept any approach in furtherance of the cause he has chosen. The argument is satisfying on a superficial level: it appears to give a clear answer to the question, while also allowing its proponents to give a reason for praising a position that instinctively appeals and denigrating one that is a source of discomfort. Thus a man who compromises on the means he employs is a reasonable individual, while a man who compromises upon the ends he seeks is a hypocrite.

Is pragmatism merely a question of doing whatever it takes to achieve one's ends, then? Some have suggested as much. Indeed, the idea that a thing or a concept should be defined in terms of its utility to the beholder was the foundation of 19th-century school of pragmatism as a philosophical approach. Its proponents argued for the pursuit of effectiveness rather than truth. Thus, from a pragmatic point of view, the *homo economicus* model – which posits economic actors as making utility-maximising decisions under conditions of perfect information – is a good model, even though we know that no real human makes decisions in such a manner, because it has a significant degree of predictive power. Unlike many epistemological trends, the idea even has a certain weight of scientific proof behind it, with computer models showing that from an evolutionary point of view, it is a poor idea to pursue truth when the key to fitness lies elsewhere. Prakash et al. have used agent-based modelling to demonstrate that when given a choice

DOI: 10.4324/9781003202721-1

between perceiving the literal truth or a beneficial fiction, the agents that follow the latter course win out and pass on their characteristics to subsequent generations.[1]

The problem with such a position, however, is that while fitness may beat truth on average, truth does not cease to exist as a result. It is the same critique as has often been levelled at Maslow's hierarchy of needs; while breathing may be more important for survival than self-actualisation, the fact remains that human history numbers millions of concrete examples of individuals who abandoned the former in pursuit of the latter. Even worse, truth exists in eight billion different versions, as everyone has his own.

So why not just find out what other people's uncompromisable ideals are and judge their level of pragmatism according to that personal yardstick? While it sounds easy, such a task has – in practice – almost always proved almost impossible.

Firstly, neither the observers nor the observed are ever entirely unbiased. Humans have an inherent universal tendency to apply emotive conjugation in all things; elevating their own motivations and denigrating others.[2] Thus, in sticking to one's guns, I am principled, you are inflexible, and he is being pig-headed; in making a compromise, I am adaptable, you are irresolute, and he is an out-and-out hypocrite. What's more, even if everyone resolves to be entirely honest in stating their ranked preferences, often they are not entirely sure what these are until they are tasked with making a real-world decision concerning them. It is more or less impossible for anyone – including the decider himself – to judge whether he's being truly pragmatic or not. So should any study of pragmatism be abandoned?

At the individual level, possibly, but state preferences are much more transparent, and this book is about state preferences as much as individual ones. Like any organisation, a state's primary goal is to perpetuate its own existence. While they may also have ideals or principles, continued existence is the key to the realisation of all other goals. A state that compromises its ideals and survives as a result is pragmatic. A state that sticks rigidly to dogma and is eliminated is not.

So the problem is solved. Can we end the book here?

Unfortunately, not, because states themselves are made up of human actors with the same tricky nested tiers of motivations and preferences described earlier. A state cannot decide to sacrifice principles for continued existence; it sacrifices principles for continued existence because a collective of individuals with confused and unknowable preference rankings have made that decision on its behalf.

The point of this book, then, is to work out why people who might be pragmatic or unpragmatic in their everyday lives, occasionally come together in the context of a state and decide to take it down the route

ensuring the ~~states~~ survival even if it means abandoning its values → pragmatic states should chose pragmatism> ideology?

of either pragmatism or ideology. What are the institutional constraints or freedoms given to them, and what incentives are at play in affecting their decisions? Why do some situations encourage pragmatism on the part of state decision-makers, while others encourage them to cling ever more tightly to ideology, even at the risk of their states and potentially their lives?

This book is an attempt to answer that question in an academically rigorous yet practically relevant manner, with two main intellectual contributions:

(1) The Pragmatism in the Policy Process Model, which is a fusion of neo-classical realism (international relations) and policy cycle (public policy) theories, describes what pragmatism looks like at different stages of the foreign policy process (agenda-setting, formulation, decision-making, implementation and evaluation), as well as a description of dynamics of structural and agential factors that form the underlying context behind any foreign policy at a specific point in time.

(2) The Description of Varieties of Pragmatism, which will use thick descriptions to show how pragmatism looks like in the foreign policy decisions made in the US, China and Singapore. Emphasis will be given to how pragmatic behaviour is observed, but might be influenced by different contextual factors: in the US, checks and balances, China with the influence of personalities and socio-political culture, and Singapore with the influence of geography and survival pressures. The cases (specific foreign policy decisions) are selected to describe the general phenomenon of pragmatism as observed at different stages of the policy process (unit of analysis: moments, as opposed to individual, institution or country), whilst noting the limits of causal explanations as even when interviewing practitioners involved in specific foreign policy decisions, it is impossible to be certain that the information received is an accurate representation of the facts. There remains a risk of practitioners offering *post-hoc* ? rationalisations to preserve their legacy.

This is the first effort in the field to construct a foreign policy conceptual framework from a combined international relations and public policy perspective and in a holistic manner. This conceptual framework, providing context and process, accounts for how policymakers perceive pragmatism, and is innovative in three aspects: Firstly, it fuses international relations and public policy to observe foreign policy-making from an actor–system perspective. Secondly, its holistic nature incorporates existing foreign policy analysis theories prevalent in international relations. Thirdly, the process part can be considered a revised version of Mintz's poliheuristic model, which states that leaders will first satisfy themselves by dropping far-fetched alternatives, before focusing on detailed rational analysis of the few final options. This pragmatism model extends this model further, to add the 'step zero' of broad strategic analysis of the situation that is needed at the start, before selection and cost–benefit analysis.

It challenges three received ideas in existing international relations discourse, which is plagued by binary thinking: realist versus liberal, ideology versus pragmatism, grand strategy versus pragmatism.

The first myth pertains to contextual problem-solving and considers the opposite of realism to be liberalism. There is quite an extensive literature on this idea, stemming from the inter-war debate, including commentaries attacking it as a false dichotomy. When faced with a problem, a policymaker will often use any and all methods to solve the problem. If realism and liberalism are considered to be methods, then it is appropriate to infer that policymakers will use realism or liberalism or a combination of the two, as the situation demands. As such, there is no realism versus liberalism dichotomy.

The second received idea sees the opposite of pragmatism as ideology. Several books have been written on the US Cold War foreign policy juxtaposing crusaders and pragmatists. However, this dichotomy is unable to account for later American foreign policy pundits' assertion that 'it is our national interest [pragmatic] to export our democracy [ideology], national destiny, and politics of liberty'.

The third and most significant false dichotomy is that of grand strategy versus pragmatism. Four distinct waypoints on the continuum of pragmatism can be identified and described: non-pragmatism, Small-P pragmatism (for personal, party or regime sub-national interest), Big-P pragmatism (for national interest) and strategic pragmatism. Most leaders' positions fall somewhere between non-pragmatism and Big-P pragmatism. Strategic pragmatism is significant because of its emphasis on systematic and rigorous analysis of the strategic situation so as to derive a grand strategy. This is the key difference between strategic pragmatism and pragmatism: strategic pragmatism's emphasis is on grand strategy and its derivation through rigorous analysis (with systems and long-term thinking) and pragmatically implementing the grand strategy with adjustments according to reality. Without the 'strategic', both forms of pragmatism still imply conducting appropriate checks during decision-making and actively adjusting and adapting according to circumstances; however, without a view of the larger grand strategy, this will likely result in knee-jerk responses and incoherence. The fusion of ends and means is achieved through strategic pragmatism.

To illustrate the various types of pragmatism, we are going to look at three particular cases: China, Singapore and the US. We deliberately chose cases centred on an Asia-Pacific axis, not because this is the only region in which pragmatism prevails, but because the rise of China and its competition for hegemony with the US is set to be the defining trend of the 21st century. Plenty of other countries and leaders have displayed pragmatism and continue to display it: one may cite post-War Germany, France under Emanuel Macron, Félix Houphouët-Boigny's Ivory Coast, modern Qatar. . . . However, any book on contemporary politics has to justify itself to contemporary audiences, and contemporary audiences are primarily interested in the situations that are most likely to affect them. While it is useful to have a cross-cultural comparison (given that previous works on the topic have tended to focus on a single cultural region), ideally this comparison should be one that is relevant and interesting for the highest possible number of people. For these reasons, we selected Asia-Pacific cases.

Our three country cases – China (section 2), Singapore (section 3) and the US (section 4) – show that while pragmatism can be a product of individual leaders' preferences shaped by structural factors (history, geography, culture), it only becomes a long-term tendency when the policy process (accounting also for the interaction between agents and realistic assumptions of misperceptions and groupthink) is structured to support Pragmatism.

The China case shows pragmatic leaders fighting to emerge from an ideological context, only able to take a pragmatic stance abroad when powerful enough to escape ideological constraints at home. The Singapore case shows how leaders may adopt a pragmatic stance as a product of outside pressures, but that over time their pragmatic decisions come in time to form the basis for a quasi-ideological superstructure. Finally, the US example shows how a system may be structured such that the actions of non-pragmatic individuals cancel each other out in the long run, producing a system with broadly pragmatic outcomes. While the US electoral system may push politicians to adopt ideological stances on the campaign trail, the checks and balances system ensures that they become more pragmatic when subjected to the pressures of office. These varieties of pragmatism illuminate how pragmatism is defined and works (or does not) in these countries, and why so, based on proxy first-hand perspective from interviews with a total of 121 practitioners and academics from the countries studied, to give a first-hand perspective. (Though it should be noted that practitioners may not speak openly due to a desire to preserve their legacy from a spirit of post hoc justification, or memory lapses.) Interviewees were recruited according to a snowball sampling method, and interviewed following a questionnaire so as to render comparison between responses easier. The list of interviewees is provided at the end of the book, along with the questionnaire used. The interviews served to provide key research points, and also deep background information.

Pragmatism is a skill (acumen and state of being), rather than a universal attribute or 'thing to do'. The mere fact of establishing it as a goal can serve to weaken one's ability to pursue it, as an idealised vision of pragmatism itself becomes merely another distracting ideology. Rather than relying on the preferences of a given individual or merely instructing a set of disparate individuals to favour pragmatism, the book argues that a system that is strategically pragmatic in the long run creates strategically pragmatic decisions at an aggregate level informed by long-term thinking and grand strategy, even if each individual decision is biased in one way or another, and pragmatically implements it to fruition with adjustments and reversals, as needed. A pragmatic system is one in which it does not just rely on individuals being pragmatic, but also a system that supports 'being pragmatic' so that the long-term overall trend is one of pragmatism.

Notes

1 Donald D. Hoffman, Manish Singh and Chetan Prakash (2015). "The Interface Theory of Perception." *Psychonomic Bulletin & Review*, Vol. 22, No. 6, pp. 1480–1506.
2 Thomas Holtgraves (2004). "Social Desirability and Self-Reports: Testing Models of Socially Desirable Responding." *Personality and Social Psychology Bulletin*, Vol. 30, No. 2, pp. 161–172.

Part I
What is pragmatism?

2 Fitness beats truth
Towards a definition of pragmatism

"I don't know what you mean by 'glory',"

– Alice said

Humpty Dumpty smiled contemptuously. "Of course you don't – till I tell you. I meant 'there's a nice knock-down argument for you!'"
"But 'glory' doesn't mean 'a nice knock-down argument',"

– Alice objected

"When I use a word," Humpty Dumpty said, in rather a scornful tone, "it means just what I choose it to mean – neither more nor less."

– Lewis Carroll

While it is normal to see fuzzy moral terms being used imprecisely in everyday and even high-stakes political contexts, "pragmatism" is interesting insofar as the lack of clarity regarding its precise meaning persists even in academia, unlike other terms – "liberalism", "significant", "deviance" – that are used vaguely in ordinary conversation but have clearly defined academic meanings. The early representatives of pragmatism as an epistemological movement (Charles Pierce et al.) put forward precise defining features of their approach:

- All knowledge rests on non-inferential foundations;
- Theories should be evaluated on the basis of utility rather than truth;
- Anti-nominalism.

Neopragmatism à la Richard Rorty, by contrast, focuses on the linguistic side of pragmatism, and the idea that the meaning of words is a function of their usage, rather than – for example – their dictionary definition.

DOI: 10.4324/9781003202721-3

Despite a flourishing literature covering philosophical pragmatism, the philosophical interpretations of pragmatism, whether the Charles Peirce, William James, James Dewey (classical) versions, or the Richard Rorty et al. version, are generally seen as being too 'philosophical' and abstract to be useful for policy-making. It is a rare politician who wonders whether he is guilty of nominalism or a priorism when making a decision, after all.

On the other hand, vernacular views of pragmatism tend to be vague and context-dependent. It is rare that an author, in either public policy or international-relations literature, applies the ideas therein as originally intended. Instead, their discussions of pragmatism often tend to refer to a fuzzy and unscientific definition that the reader is supposed to infer from context. Indeed, it would arguably be inappropriate to do so, since no politician takes abstract theories of knowledge into account when making real-world decisions.

From a practical politics-and-international-relations point of view, various attempts have been made to study pragmatism as a concept by international-relations theory with two books and one journal volume on it in the last 15 years. As we have already noted, aspects of philosophical pragmatism offer promising insights for the field of international relations, but the theories are often too abstract to be used by policymakers.

Millennium Journal, Volume 31, in 2002 explored the theoretical possibilities of pragmatism as an alternative paradigm, and Harry Bauer and Elizabetta Brighi followed up with an edited volume, Pragmatism in IR. This was a European effort to explore the pragmatic approach to IR with the aim of 'transcend[ing] the variety of well-worn debates that run the risk of paralysing the field', with a focus on specific historical practices.

Shane Ralston's edited volume, *Philosophical Pragmatism and International Relations,* represents the latest effort to describe and explore the nexus of philosophical pragmatism as an alternative paradigm in international relations. Some case studies on pragmatism in international relations have often referred to the US, from the broad-based *American Diplomacy and the Pragmatic Tradition,* to a recent work on Obama's Pragmatism. The problem is that none of these studies have produced a concise and precise definition of the term that has carried enough weight to "stick" among both academics and their subjects. Though all contained interesting insights, and the author is extremely grateful to such publications for informing and guiding the present study, the use of the term "pragmatism" has nevertheless remained fuzzy. No one definition has been able to predominate to such an extent that writers may be criticised for deviating from it (as in the case of "liberalism", "significant" and "deviance" mentioned earlier). Scholars thus remain free to construct their own definitions, or simply to use the word without giving a particular definition at all.

Moreover, the term "pragmatism" tends to be overused and under-theorised. A quick survey of the literature on pragmatism in foreign policy fails to produce a consensus even on basic issues such as whether "pragmatic" should be considered complimentary or pejorative. Often, pragmatism is used loosely to connote whatever the author wishes. A quick survey of 48 existing publications on pragmatic foreign policy reveals an inconsistent usage of the term. Countries involved included Canada, the UK, Latin America, Taiwan, Russia, Japan, India, Iran, the US, China, and various EU, Middle Eastern, and African countries, all of which were labelled pragmatic at some point. Almost half of the articles (23), that describe a country's foreign policy as pragmatic, do not define pragmatism.[1] See pg. 30–33 for selected list of existing literature.

Perhaps, pragmatism is often defined *via negativa*, by excluding phenomena that it definitely is not. Indeed, this approach has a strong appeal: not only is defining unpragmatic behaviour far easier, but "unpragmatism" can be proven using scientific methods, unlike the varying degrees of pragmatism and quasi-pragmatism.

In short, unpragmatism can be said to be any decision that values deontological principles over long-term goals. This is hard to assess in the case of individual behaviour, since individuals' long-term goals all differ and tend to be hard to pin down and rank, even for the individuals themselves. Fortunately for our purposes, organisations' long-term goals are all identical: the perpetuation of the organisation. Thus, any state that acts in ways detrimental to its own survival can confidently be said to be unpragmatic. Probably the most famous example of such behaviour would be the actions of the Nazi leadership during the later stages of World War II, when they continued to divert resources towards the extermination of the Jews despite knowing that it hampered the war effort and thus the survival prospects of their state.

However, Pragmatism is a problem-solving approach, an art. By understanding pragmatism from a practitioner perspective, we aim to add value to international relations and public policy disciplines. Most practitioners interviewed in this research stated that they did not explicitly refer to any international-relations theory to guide their policy-making processes. A foreign policy problem occurred, and they were simply trying to solve it. Pragmatism for them was a goal-oriented problem-solving approach. From their perspective, pragmatism is defined as 'what works' to achieve the desired end-state, with an emphasis on robust fact-based analysis, strategy, and flexibility during implementation. The pragmatist is not fixated on any ideology but rather uses any method that works in the context as a strategy to achieve desired goals.

Pragmatism as compromise

If we take the line of argument that pragmatism is a problem-solving approach, then perhaps a *via positiva* definition of pragmatism is compromise. Compromise at the decision-making stage is often evidenced by a willingness to accept the imperfections of one's situation. Compromise is often essentially an acceptance of scarcity: while every state has high-reaching goals, these tend to be constrained by the available resources, and hence compromises must be made. Building a new hospital here means that I cannot build a new university there.[2] It can also be seen in the willingness to recognise past failures and changing circumstances. If the situation has changed and/or a strategy is not working, compromise implies its rejection or adaptation.[3]

Epistemologically and ontologically, openness to compromise is linked to the willingness to acknowledge fallibility and imperfect information. In fashionable terms, one may say that it is based on an epistemological acceptance of the precepts of complexity theory, accepting that ideas that may have been adapted to yesterday's circumstances may not be adapted to today's, though one's goals may not have changed.

Consequently, this implies the use of inductive methods, since under such assumptions a deductive approach will have a sell-by-date, and become increasingly inaccurate over time.[4] If Pragmatism is a problem-solving approach, then there is no fixed 'textbook' universal answer, it will necessarily be a skill and acumen where its right application to context matters.

If compromise is the only *via positiva* proof of pragmatism, it is then essential to describe the ways in which political compromise may manifest itself, and observe examples of compromise. If a policy has never raised a question of conflicts between deontological principles and long-term goals, then it is impossible for an observer to judge whether or not it is pragmatic. As such, the book will highlight examples of compromise (or its absence) in foreign policy of China, Singapore, the US, and analyses the process by which the decision to compromise (or not) was made by the individuals responsible.

It is important to note that states do not themselves make decisions. Any state is made up of human actors with the same tricky nested tiers of motivations and preferences described earlier. A state cannot decide to sacrifice principles for continued existence; it sacrifices principles for continued existence because a collection of individuals with confused and unknowable preference rankings made that decision on its behalf.

We are also going to take particular care to evaluate pragmatism only at the level of the decision, rather than the individual, institution or country. As we shall demonstrate in the country cases below, the behaviour of individuals and institutions is simply too variable and contingent of other contextual factors to be able to label one pragmatic and the other non-pragmatic in a definitive manner. The same individual may make a pragmatic decision one minute and an ideological one the next. Moreover, an individual may perform ideology or Big-P pragmatism for Small-P pragmatic reasons, making it exceptionally difficult to distinguish forms and motivations. At the decision level, on the other hand, the willingness of a given actor to compromise can be isolated and studied, enabling a clearer judgement as to whether the decision constitutes an example of Small-P or Big-P pragmatism, or genuine ideological belief.

A more detailed study of pragmatism in international relations would require thicker descriptions of how and why pragmatism works in a large *N* survey of cases. Specifically, it would require researchers to identify pragmatic and non-pragmatic decisions made by practitioners, and compare the factors affecting each, as well as their results.

However, given the abstractness of existing research of Pragmatism in International Relations and the paucity of research on Pragmatism at the foreign policy level, this book will seek to operationalise pragmatism in international relations through understanding how pragmatism works in specific states' foreign policy, creating the beginnings of an internal taxonomy of forms of pragmatism. In this enterprise, we begin from the premise that pragmatism is always an inherently context-dependent phenomenon – hence decisions may be called pragmatic, but individuals or states cannot. In order to define and explore the term, therefore, it is necessary to look at the contextual factors that trigger or prevent particular forms of pragmatism. As such, if we are going to construct a precise and rigorous definition of pragmatism for use in the public policy and international relations context, we must proceed in a properly pragmatic way from concrete case studies to reliable generalisations.

Before that, let's illustrate Pragmatism in finer detail.

Notes

1 For reference, the full list is provided at the end of this chapter.
2 Interview with former Singapore Foreign Minister S. Dhanabalan on 18 January 2017.
3 Interview with former US Defense Department Assistant Secretary for International Security Affairs, Prof Joseph S. Nye Jr. on 9 May 2017.
4 Interview with former US Defence Department Assistant Secretary for International Security Affairs, Amb Charles W. (Chas) Freeman Jr. on 1 June 2017.

3 Big-P and Small-P pragmatism, strategic pragmatism and grand strategy

While the idea of "pragmatism of means" and "pragmatism of ends" is a familiar one, it is strangely lacking in everyday utility, mainly due to the universal human tendency towards emotive conjugation, as described earlier. Simply put, everyone wishes to lay claim to pragmatism of means, and no one will admit to pragmatism of ends. This – in combination with the difficulties inherent in analysing others' motivations – makes it difficult to assign either definition to any given action with 100% confidence. Instead, we chose a different – and we hope more practically relevant distinction – that of "Small-P" and "Big-P" pragmatism. These concepts are not taken from any particular work on the topic, but rather are the product of our efforts to amalgamate the most useful aspects of existing definitions into broad categories with practical applications, relying upon interviews with practitioners and experts to better mirror their experience of the process.[1]

On the pragmatism/non-pragmatism continuum, we identify four specific forms of pragmatism (see Table 3.1). Please note that these are not taken from any particular work on the topic, but rather are the product of our efforts to amalgamate the most useful aspects of existing definitions into broad categories with practical applications, relying upon interviews with practitioners and experts to better mirror their experience of the process. What we are referring to as "Small-P pragmatism" is more often referred to as expediency in the literature:

Small-P pragmatism

It is a given that the vast majority of politicians are pragmatic (Small-P), when it comes to achieving the desired outcome of remaining in power. They are pragmatic because of personal, political, regime or party survival. While pragmatic behaviour may be observed (such as fact-based analysis, flexible implementation), such Small-P pragmatism may easily degrade into expediency, wherein a problem solved in the short term creates more

DOI: 10.4324/9781003202721-4

Table 3.1 The pragmatism continuum

	Non-pragmatic	Small-P	Big-P	Strategic pragmatism
Analysis	Wish-based analysis	Fact-based analysis	Fact-based analysis	Fact-based analysis
Emphasis	Dualism with an emphasis on principle	Dualism with an emphasis on pragmatism	Duality – Principled with pragmatic execution	Duality – Principled with pragmatic execution
Strategy	No grand strategy even when expedient	No grand strategy	No grand strategy	Grand strategy
Implementation	Fixed implementation	Flexible implementation	Flexible implementation	Flexible implementation
Application	Universalism	Contextualism	Contextualism	Contextualism
Example	Mao Zedong great leap forward, cultural revolution	Nixon rapprochement with China	Deng with the US over Taiwan; One country two systems	Singapore–China relations

problems in the long term. For the purposes of this study, Small-P pragmatism will be considered to be any decision in which a politician compromises upon pre-established principles in order to advance his career or preserve his life. In practice, this often overlaps with the concept of "pragmatism of ends". Such a politician is willing to accept an outcome that he knows to be sub-par for the country, as long as it assures his own survival. One example of this would be Deng Xiaoping's willingness to pay lip service to communist ideology to ensure his own survival, despite not believing it to be the best policy for the country.

Big-P pragmatism

Big-P pragmatism focuses on getting things done for the national or supranational interest. Big-P Pragmatism solves the problem more thoroughly and in the long term. It often involves policy innovation exercising both/and thinking and looking at win–win solutions (duality). It seeks a balance of principle and pragmatism during implementation. This study will cover Small-P pragmatism, but its main focus is on this type of Big-P pragmatism. In Big-P pragmatic decisions, principles may be compromised; but this is done because it promises to bring advantages that will benefit the nation as a whole, not merely an individual or a party. As we shall see in the following chapters, Big-P and Small-P pragmatism can either conflict or reinforce each other. If a politician is forced to espouse ideological positions in which he does not believe to ensure his own survival, and which are also detrimental to the national interest, this is a case of Small-P pragmatism entering into conflict with Big-P pragmatism. On the other hand, when circumstances oblige a politician to make Big-P pragmatic decisions in order to be able to produce good results and thereby ensure his own survival (a Small-P goal), that is an example of the two types of pragmatism reinforcing one another. Thus, for example, Deng Xiaoping's eventual economic reforms were necessary to create the growth necessary to ensure his own political survival, but also benefited the nation as a whole.

Strategic pragmatism and grand strategy

Grand strategy and pragmatism are not antithetical, and can co-exist. Strategic pragmatism exists when one has a rigorously devised grand strategy (potentially guided by principles/ideology) that is realistic in its analysis and policy options, and flexibly implemented to adapt to the situation, including tactical adjustments and strategic reversals, to achieve the desired vision and goals. Without an overarching grand strategy, it is likely that feedback loops will lead to knee-jerk responses. This is the gold standard for Pragmatism. For parsimony's sake, it can be summarised in terms of five key features:

Realistic analysis: fact-based analysis of reality; reality as it is, not as one wishes.

Duality: striving for policy innovation or hybrids; breaks the either/or construct, moving towards a both/and construct (duality) where co-existence, mutual wins are possible and desired. This combines principles and pragmatism. Fitzgerald aptly surmised the essence of duality: "The test of first-rate intelligence is the ability to hold two opposed in mind at the same time and still retain the ability to function."[2]

Grand strategy: having a grand strategy to achieve desired strategic vision. Grand strategy has to demonstrate foresight (scenario planning) and insight (systems thinking) in analysis, and long-term planning to achieve long-lasting goals. This is the differentiating factor between Strategic Pragmatism and Pragmatism.

Flexibility in implementation: adopting an experimental, trial-and-error approach during implementation which acknowledges that the initial plan may not be perfect. This entails tactical adjustments, operational changes, strategic policy reversals and tight feedback loops. This is a response to the dynamism inherent in complex reality.

Contextualism: having a propensity to reject universal application of particular principles/ideology regardless of context. Having a sensitivity to context allows one to better solve problems in a systemic and long-lasting manner.

At the opposite end of the scale, non-pragmatism is directed by ideology: driven by wish-based analysis and with principle predominating over being realistic when the two enter into conflict.

Notes

1 Interview with Lou Marinoff, 11 May 2017, interview with Chiang Chie Foo, 2 March 2017, interview with Ravi Menon, 8 February 2017, interview with Marc Grossman, 10 July 2017.
2 F. Scott Fitzgerald (1925). *Great Gatsby.* New York: Charles Scribner's Sons.

4 Agential and structural factors of (pragmatic) production

If this book is to be useful to policymakers, then the systematic analysis of different aspects of pragmatism must be inserted into a pragmatism in policy process framework, that make sense from a practitioner perspective. This framework accounts for the dynamics of agential and structural factors at work that form the underlying context behind any foreign policy at a specific point in time. The Pragmatism in the Policy Process Framework is a fusion of neoclassical realism (international relations) and policy cycle (public policy) theories and describes what pragmatism looks like at different stages of the foreign policy process (agenda-setting, formulation, decision-making, implementation and evaluation).

Pragmatism as a problem-solving approach necessitates the right application of Pragmatism in Policy Process to the context. Pragmatism cannot be applied universally in a vacuum, devoid of context. Pragmatism as a problem-solving approach is hence necessarily context-dependent. The context of foreign policy problem hence becomes important. Context includes agential and structural factors working in iterative interaction. A clearer understanding of these factors helps policymakers navigate the situation to achieve desired policy outcomes.

This approach puts the leader(s) at centre stage and looks at the agential and structural factors influencing their worldview(s). Structural factors exist at different levels and can be observed from different disciplinary perspectives.

In terms of these factors, there are at least four levels of analyses that can be adopted: international, regional, national and local. International factors include international institutions such as the United Nations, as well as international law and agreements. Regional factors cover regional institutions as the European Union (EU) or the Association of Southeast Asian Nations (ASEAN), as well as the regulations and agreements between states in a particular region, among others. The national level includes domestic politics and institutions, while the local level focuses on local politics and institutions.

DOI: 10.4324/9781003202721-5

At these levels of analysis, different disciplinary perspectives interact. History, geography and culture all influence actors to different extents and form a baseline for leaders' worldviews. So, for example, China's 'century of humiliation' created a strong desire to become a great power once more, and fuelled anxiety over territorial integrity. At the international, regional and national levels, prior policy often sets the policy context in which policy adjustments, adaptations or even reversals happen. Moreover, prior policy can play an enabling or constraining role in the making of any new policies.

Agential factors are different from structural factors insofar as that agents have volition and are able to determine a course of action, and carry it out. Domestic institutions vary by country but common actors include politicians, bureaucrats, corporate interests, civil society. The actors' roles are self-explanatory but the configurations and influence of different actors differ by country, thus linking political systems and pragmatism/ non-pragmatism.

Agential and structural factors interact in different ways to impact each other at different parts of the policy process. Different actors have different interests and different abilities to influence different parts of the process. Therein lies the art of compromise and even policy innovation to achieve win–win policy outcomes. Bounded rationality, satisficing and imperfect information are deemed as realistic assumptions that fuel misperceptions and groupthink, which are human limits that must be taken into account during interaction of structural and agential factors.

Agential and structural factors interact in different ways to impact each other and different parts of the policy process. Technically, different actors have different volitions and the ability to influence different parts of the process. In the spirit of parsimony, our model only seeks to articulate the more dominant influences in this web of relationships between the context and the policies that it produces. These are:

(1) *The influence of structure on agency.* Structural factors function as enablers and/or constraints on actors (leader and domestic institutions). The extent of their impact on actors will vary by actor, but personal experience will likely create a more indelible impact. Lee Kuan Yew's personal experience of World War II, for example, left an indelible impression that defence is of utmost importance and a sovereign state cannot rely on other countries for its defence. Hence, building a strong and credible defence force was a key task from Singapore's independence till the present day.

(2) *The influence of cognitive psychology on individuals and groups.* All leaders are vulnerable to misperceptions. Regardless of the cohesiveness of a group, when there is more than one person, there is likely

to be disagreement because everyone's interpretation of facts can be different due to human cognitive limits. All groups of actors (corporate, bureaucracy, civil society, experts, politicians) will be liable to group dynamics that vary from groupthink to the bargaining and conflict displayed in the kind of groups described in Allison's Third Model of Governmental Politics. Applying the principle of duality, the crux is how to guard against both and benefit from creative tension produced by rigorous debate while retaining unity.

(3) *The influence of agency on process.* At the risk of generalisation, agenda-setting is often the prerogative of the dominant leader. Policy formulation is largely a collective effort with weightage on the bureaucrats who support politicians/leaders. Decision-making is also the final prerogative of the dominant leader, though group dynamics in the discussions leading to the decision may affect it, and therein lies the impact of group dynamics. In public policy literature, implementation tends to be the prerogative of bureaucrats. However, on the international stage, some of the highest-level processes are conducted by high-level politicians at the head-of-state and head-of-government levels. In public policy literature, evaluation is the stage at which experts and civil society have the most scope to play an active role.

Our three country sections focusing on China, Singapore and the US show that while pragmatism can be a product of individual leaders' preferences, as shaped by structural factors, plus history, geography and culture, it only becomes a long-term tendency when the policy process is structured to support pragmatism.

Moreover, while pragmatism may be a good goal for any state to aim at, the mere fact of establishing it as a goal can serve to weaken one's ability to pursue it, as an idealised vision of pragmatism itself becomes merely another distracting ideology. Rather than relying on the preferences of a given individual or merely instructing a set of disparate individuals to favour pragmatism, we argue that a system that is pragmatic in the long run creates pragmatic decisions at an aggregate level, even if each individual decision is biased in one way or another. A pragmatic system is one in which it does not just rely on individuals making pragmatic choices (as a skill and acumen), but also a system that supports more pragmatic choices (made from skill and acumen) so that the long-term overall trend is one of pragmatism.

5 Pragmatism in policy process framework

Existing context-process models (international relations)

Our Pragmatism in Policy Process Framework seeks to present how pragmatism works (or should work) from a practitioner perspective. When an international relations perspective is required, we use the basic assumptions of the neoclassical realist model of foreign policy, as a useful base of context-process model, with some modifications to factor in imperfect rationality and individual subjectivity.

The neoclassical realist model of foreign policy states that systemic incentives (independent variables) drive internal factors (intervening variables) which lead to a foreign policy.

This model has been chosen as a base for three reasons. Firstly, it is the most comprehensive model of foreign policy which synthesises various existing micro and macro theories of foreign policy. It is a hybrid of (structure) neo/structural realism (later split into offensive and defensive realism) and (agency) agent-centric classical realism. Secondly, neoclassical realism focuses on 'mid-range theorising to explain tangible foreign policy behaviour and patterns of grand strategic adjustment (in context), as opposed to highly abstract and general patterns of international political outcomes', making it a useful fit with the aims of this study. Lastly, it describes foreign policy as a 'process' format, and posits certain micro and macro factors of influence in a web of relationships.

This approach is easily understandable and serves as a good base as a context-process model for modification. Moreover, from a philosophically pragmatic perspective, it can be said to make broadly accurate predictions (for the time being, at least), and therefore to be a good model, even if it is possible to isolate many cases wherein individuals do not comply with its precepts. Despite this, we have taken care not to draw conclusions from this specific theory, because – as we discussed earlier – approaching the topic

DOI: 10.4324/9781003202721-6

Table 5.1 Four theories of foreign policy (Gideon Rose)

Theory	View of International System	View of Units	Causal Logic
Innenpolitik theories	unimportant	highly differentiated	internal factors → foreign policy
Defensive realism	occasionally important; anarchy's implications variable	highly differentiated	systemic incentives *or* internal factors → foreign policy (two sets of independent variables in practice, driving "natural" and "unnatural" behavior respectively)
Neoclassical realism	important; anarchy is murky	differentiated	systemic incentives (independent variable) → internal factors (intervening variables) → foreign policy
Offensive realism	very important; anarchy is Hobbesian	undifferentiated	systemic incentives → foreign policy

from a deductive perspective would be an ontological contradiction, and a denial of the precepts of complexity theory.

The policy cycle approach (public policy)

We contend that it is entirely possible for a state or an individual to behave in a pragmatic manner at one point in time or on a particular issue, and not under other circumstances. The time dimension becomes important. Hence, we split the decision-making process into stages, to better permit the isolation of pragmatic and non-pragmatic choices. The state decision-making process is generally recognised as being susceptible to being broken down into five main stages, and public policy literature has done significant work in this area: agenda-setting, policy formulation, public policy decision-making, policy implementation and policy evaluation.

The literature covering the policy cycle is extensive. Baumgartner and Jones's 'Agendas and Instability' (1993) is a classic on agenda-setting, for example. Works that are relevant across both international relations and public policy are rare, but Goldstein and Keohane (1993) provide comprehensive coverage. The policy cycle model can be relevant in foreign policy analysis. The neoclassical realist model of foreign policy states that systemic incentives (independent variable) drives internal factors (intervening variable) which leads to foreign policy. The policy cycle model adds to the internal factors a process element to better describe policy process behind foreign policy-making. As described earlier, the policy cycle is a simplified 5-step model based on Lasswell's (1956) 7-step model (intelligence, promotion, prescription, invocation, application, termination and appraisal).

In public policy literature, the policy cycle model fulfils a key role in structuring a wide range of theoretical concepts, analytical tools. The policy cycle model thus provides a heuristic device to 'enhance the understanding of complex preconditions, central factors influencing, and diverse outcomes of the policy process.'

The final outcome is the result of interaction between strategies and their implementation, with inherent unknowns that may derail the policies involved from achieving the desired outcomes. As such, it is not possible to equate 'being pragmatic' as an absolute guarantee of policy success (outcome). A policymaker can at best maintain pragmatism as a state of being (acumen) for every stage of policy process (moment) to ensure pragmatism is maximised. The ensuing section articulates what pragmatism looks like at different stages of the policy process.

Pragmatism in a policy process framework

The main contribution of this book is the Pragmatism in Policy Process framework, inspired by the existing context-process model (from

International Relations) and policy process (Public Policy) literature[1] and interviews with foreign policy practitioners (listed at the end of each chapter). Pragmatism in Policy Process framework posits that systemic factors influence agential factors interactively and iteratively (context), and it is in this underlying context that agents (as intervening variables) interact with both agents and ground reality in the policy process to make pragmatic/non-pragmatic decisions at different stages of the foreign policy process (agenda setting, formulation, decision-making, implementation and evaluation). This model seeks to create a convergence of these two disciplines through the use of practitioner testimony.

The Pragmatism in Policy Process framework seeks in the ensuing sections to articulate: (1) How pragmatism is manifested at different policy stages, (2) The dynamics of structural and agential factors in complex policy environments, (3) How the country chapters will demonstrate varieties in pragmatism (the US versus China versus Singapore) and how cases in each country demonstrate pragmatism in policy process framework in action in a descriptive manner.

We use four levels of analyses: individual, group, national and supranational, arguing that pragmatism translates to different actions in the five different stages of the foreign policy process.

(1) *National agenda-setting.* This can be done by any political actor, foreign or domestic. In practice, foreign policy tends to be reactive, so the agenda is set either by other states' actions or our own perceptions of their actions. In foreign policy, the policy process generally starts with the individual. In most cases, the dominant leader sets the foreign policy agenda, though his worldview will be affected by structural factors. Similarly, domestic institutions, and particularly civil society, can also contribute to agenda-setting. This can be done informally or formally. Preceding events may be evaluated to form the basis for 'new' agenda setting. Pragmatism in national agenda-setting means being realistic (fact-based analysis) and rational in the assessment of the situation (supranational and national environments), and acknowledging a need to respond to changing circumstances. In World War I, for example, mutual paranoia regarding neighbouring states' military capacities produced a snowballing arms build-up, an example of fact-based analysis being rejected in favour of incorrect assumptions (wish-based analysis).

(2) *National formulation.* Formulation means devising policy options to resolve the policy problem in question. Politicians, bureaucrats and experts influence foreign policy in different ways, depending on the political system. In most cases, bureaucrats tend to formulate

policy options for politicians to decide on. During formulation, cognitive, psychological and sociological factors will affect individuals and group dynamics. As such, groupthink and misperceptions are considered realistic assumptions that will plague this policy process. Pragmatism in national formulation involves noting these limits of human rationality, but seeking to overcome them through process mechanisms. Specifically, this means formulating options based on facts, rather than wishes, and due diligence to explore different possibilities. This results in an array of policy options with 'homework' done in the sense of cost–benefit analysis for each option, and even policy innovation to achieve multiple win–win objectives. At this stage, pragmatism tends to be evidenced by a willingness to consider all options, rather than to work backwards from an ideological choice that has already been fixed upon (as in the case of the Second Gulf War, when the decision to go to war was made and then "evidence" gathered to support it). At the formulation stage, all options must be considered, and a cost–benefit analysis carried out, considering policy innovations to break the gridlock.

(3) *National decision-making.* The decisions made by political, diplomatic and bureaucratic actors; decision-making decides the policy option that will be implemented. The exact decision dynamics depend on the group configuration and power dynamics in operation at the time. It is realistic to expect certain compromises between stakeholders to ensure sustainable support for the decision made. Pragmatism in national decision-making implies a rational and realistic assessment of which option will work to produce the desired policy outcome. This is where Small P will likely focus on policy outcomes desirable for personal, political, party, regime survival, while Big P will likely focus on outcomes desirable for the nation and for the longer term (more in the next chapter). Decision-making must be done in such a way as to prevent groupthink and misperceptions. This can be assisted via the cost–benefit analysis described earlier, with an eye to long-term consequences.

(4) *National implementation.* Implementation involves the execution of the policy option decided. This requires the executor to be aware of the policy intent, considerations and desired outcome. Given the unknown unknowns involved in reality, pragmatism means willingness to trial and error, adjust based on ground reality and rapid feedback loops, flexibility in navigating towards desired outcome. This largely involves compromises between evolving stakeholder concerns and the actual ground reality to work towards the desired policy outcome.

(5) <u>*National evaluation*</u>. Evaluation involves an internal assessment of what has worked and not worked for the said policy outcome. The strongest indicator of pragmatism in an evaluation is the presence of policy reversals. It demonstrates the policymaker's acceptance of fallibility, fact-based analysis of the evolving situation, willingness to be not fixated to the 'old' plan, and willingness to adjust and even make a 180-degree change to the plan if ground reality necessitates it.

This book will apply this Pragmatism in Policy Process framework in analysing the cases in the ensuing chapters. While the international dimension will not be applied, it is worth highlighting here, for completeness' sake:

(6) <u>*National implementation/International agenda-setting*</u>. In international relations, national implementation refers to the implementation of a national policy response at the supranational level. This can also be regarded as agenda-setting on the international stage, with different national foreign policy actors putting forth their national foreign policy positions. This stage is where international expectations and national positions collide. Actors' perceptions of their country's place on the international stage affect their conduct. Countries often frame their positions (both internally and externally) in ideological terms.

(7) <u>*National evaluation/International formulation*</u>. In the international formulation stage, pragmatism sets in after the national position has been declared, in the form of rapid feedback loops as part of national evaluation. It allows pragmatic policymakers to adjust their tactical positions with the knowledge of what other international actors' real interests underlying their positions are, with the aim of achieving the greatest utility (win–win for both sides). This entails willingness to trial and error, adapt and adjust to changing reality. Policy innovation and reversals are strong indicators of pragmatism.

(8) <u>*International decision-making*</u>. In the international decision-making stage, this is similar to domestic decision-making where compromise is sought through various techniques between stakeholders, with the exception that there are many diverse stakeholders in the international dimension. A pragmatic international decision is one that looks at the cost–benefit analysis and desired outcomes from the international community and for the long term.

Note

1 Valerie Hudson (2005). "Foreign Policy Analysis: Actor-Specific Theory and the Ground of International Relations." *Foreign Policy Analysis*, Vol. 1, No. 1, p. 1.

6 Varieties of pragmatism

Pragmatism being a highly contingent phenomenon, it can only have relevance in a specific context. There is no such thing as an inherently pragmatic action: the pragmatism or unpragmatism of given actions can only be judged in light of the context in which they take place. As such, to analyse given cases we adopt an approach pioneered by Peter Hall in studying varieties of capitalism.

Varieties of pragmatism

Like capitalism, pragmatism varies by country. This idea takes inspiration from the book *Varieties of Capitalism* by Peter Hall (2001),[1] which describes the different models used in Germany, Japan and Scandinavia, as influenced by their diverse legal systems, histories, cultures, and political systems. It posits that there are: (1) Liberal Market Economies (e.g., the UK and the US) (influence of market mechanisms); (2) Coordinated Market Economies (e.g., Germany, Japan, Scandinavia) (influence of non-market mechanisms such as government, trade unions and plurality of actors) enabled by different institutional factors such as legal, history, culture, political system amongst others.

Similarly, the country chapters seek to describe different country 'models' of pragmatism. The 'models' are not in a definitive sense of China's pragmatism, but in this particular 'fixated' way, period.

The 'Varieties of Pragmatism' here refers to different country 'models' of pragmatism where we seek to understand the contextual enablers where structural and agential factors interact iteratively, describe the unique peculiarities of each country's pragmatism and identify dominant enablers that account for varieties of pragmatism across the US, China and Singapore. As such, the three country chapters are intended as a descriptive account to capture how pragmatism is manifested in different ways (the way Varieties of Capitalism illustrates how different countries have different models of Capitalism).

DOI: 10.4324/9781003202721-7

The aim is not to produce a predictive model, nor a generalisable theory of causality, but rather to clarify a concept that is generally applied vaguely. This remains a vital first step before any form of credible causality modelling can be conceived. The unit of analysis, as mentioned earlier, is that of specific decisions with emphasis that each decision can have different policy stages where pragmatism is manifested differently. We will illustrate how pragmatism has been observed in specific foreign policy decisions (case). Therein, we apply the Pragmatism in Policy Process framework to these cases to see how pragmatism was applied in different stages (moments of the case) of the foreign policy process, noting that not all decisions will be pragmatic, from agenda setting to formulation to decision-making to implementation to evaluation. Thick descriptions of individual pragmatic decisions increase the depth and precision of the definition that emerges.

This includes discussions of Small-P, Big-P and strategic pragmatism at the case and moment levels. This breaks the tendency to assign pragmatic/non-pragmatic labels to countries and leaders, but instead to specific moments of policy process. We argue that it is futile to label a country or leader as pragmatic or non-pragmatic, because they make decisions based on specific context of foreign policy events. Pragmatism is a contextual attribute. Hypothetical counter-factual scenarios of non-pragmatism are avoided since context is important to any application of pragmatic problem-solving approach. Similarly, the focus is on *via positiva* (what pragmatism looks like), rather *via negativa* (what Pragmatism is not) descriptions, hence the focus on positive instances of pragmatism in any part of the policy process.

Our three country cases: China (section 2), Singapore (section 3) and the US (section 4) shows that while pragmatism can be a product of individual leaders' preferences shaped by structural factors (history, geography, culture), it only becomes a long-term tendency when the policy process (accounting also for the interaction between agents and realistic assumptions of misperceptions and groupthink) is structured to support Pragmatism.

Moreover, while pragmatism may be a good goal for any state to aim at, the mere fact of establishing it as a goal can serve to weaken one's ability to pursue it, as an idealised vision of pragmatism itself becomes merely another distracting ideology. Pragmatism is a skill, rather than a universal attribute. Rather than relying on the preferences of a given individual or merely instructing a set of disparate individuals to favour pragmatism, the book argues that a system that is pragmatic in the long run creates pragmatic decisions at an aggregate level, even if each individual decision is biased in one way or another. A pragmatic system is one in which it does not just rely on individuals making pragmatic choices (as a skill and acumen), but also a system that supports more pragmatic choices (made from skill and acumen) so that the long-term overall trend is one of pragmatism.

Pragmatism in China, Singapore and the United States

To illustrate the theories described earlier, this book will take three examples of pragmatism in politics – from the US, China and Singapore – and analyses them in depth, looking at the institutions and incentives that pushed the state decision-makers towards a pragmatic position, as well as those that intervened in the opposite direction.

These three cases were chosen for their ability to provide examples of the ways in which pragmatism and unpragmatism interact, being the product of both agents and structures. The China case shows pragmatic leaders fighting to emerge from an ideological context, only able to take a pragmatic stance abroad when powerful enough to escape ideological constraints at home. The Singapore case shows how leaders may adopt a pragmatic stance as a result of outside pressures, but that, over time their pragmatic decisions come in time to form the basis for a quasi-ideological superstructure. Finally, the US example shows how a system may be structured such that the actions of non-pragmatic individuals cancel each other out in the long run, producing a system with broadly pragmatic outcomes. While the US electoral system may push politicians to adopt ideological stances on the campaign trail, the checks and balances system ensures that they become more pragmatic when subjected to the pressures of office.

The area studies approach towards understanding the US, China and Singapore helps to examine why and how pragmatism is defined and works (or does not) in these countries, to illuminate different varieties of. These country cases were based largely on interviews with a total of 121 practitioners and academics from the countries studied, to give a first-hand perspective.

It is important to note that – as mentioned earlier – the unit of analysis in each case is the decision, rather than the individual, institutions or country. As we shall see in the country cases below, the behaviour of individuals and institutions is simply too variable and contingent of other contextual factors to be able to label one pragmatic and the other non-pragmatic in a definitive manner. The same individual may make a pragmatic decision one minute and an ideological one the next.

Upon these foundations, it will set out a conceptual framework to identify varieties of pragmatism in foreign policy, with the key points and advice for future practitioners laid out in the conclusion. By doing this, it aims to provide help to decision-makers elsewhere on how they cannot merely try to take a more pragmatic stance themselves, but also redesign their organisation to make sure that everyone in it is just that little bit more pragmatic.

Selected Existing Literature on Pragmatism (under/undefined) in Foreign Policy

Abadi, Jacob (1999). 'Pragmatism and Rhetoric in Yemen's Policy Towards Israel', *Journal of Third World Studies*, Vol. 16, No. 2, pp. 95–118.

Abadi, Jacob (2002). 'Algeria's Policy Towards Israel: Pragmatism and Rhetoric', *Middle East Journal*, Vol. 56, No. 4, p. 616.

Amstutz, Mark R. (2014). *Evangelicals and American Foreign Policy*, New York: Oxford University Press.

Baylis, John (1993). *The Diplomacy of Pragmatism: Britain and the Formation of NATO, 1942–49*, Basingstoke: Macmillan.

Chauvin, Lucien (2014). 'Andean Peru: Limits of Pragmatism', in *Latin Finance*, Coral Gables: European Money Trading Limited.

Chen Jie (1992). *Ideology in US Foreign Policy: Case Studies in US China Policy*, Westport, CT: Praeger.

Chen Jie (2002). *Foreign Policy of the New Taiwan: Pragmatic Diplomacy in Southeast Asia*, Cheltenham: Edward Elgar.

Ching, Frank (1993). 'Pragmatism Is the Hallmark of Peking's Foreign Policy', *Far Eastern Economic Review*, p. 31.

Cornell, Katherine F. (1996). 'From Patronage to Pragmatism: Central Europe and the United States', *World Policy Journal*, Vol. 13, p. 91.

Cornell, Svante E. (2001). 'Iran and the Caucasus: The Triumph of Pragmatism Over Ideology', *Global Dialogue*, Vol. 3, Nos. 2–3, p. 91.

Coufoudakis, Van (1982). 'Ideology and Pragmatism in Greek Foreign Policy', *Current History*, Vol. 81, No. 479, pp. 426–432.

Crabb Jr., Cecil V. (1989). *American Diplomacy and the Pragmatic Tradition*, London: Louisiana State University Press.

Dagli, Murat (2013). 'The Limits of Ottoman Pragmatism', *History and Theory*, Vol. 52, May, pp. 202–203.

Davis, Jonathan E. (2011). 'From Ideology to Pragmatism: China's Position on Humanitarian Intervention in the Post Cold War Era', *Vanderbilt Journal of Transnational Law*, Vol. 44, No. 2, pp. 217–283.

Dettmer, Jamie (2000). 'Albright Praises Putin's Pragmatism', *Insight*, pp. 16–17.

Dwyer, Rob (2013). 'The Pragmatism of Mexico's Agustin Carstens', *Euromoney*.

Engerman, David C. (2006). 'John Dewey and the Soviet Union: Pragmatism Meets Revolution', *Modern Intellectual History*, Vol. 3, No. 1, pp. 35–36.

Fares, Seme Taleb (2007). 'The Oil Pragmatism: The Brazil-Iraq Relations', *Revista Brasileira de Política Internacional*, Vol. 50, No. 2, pp. 129–145.

Feinsilver, Julie M. (2010). 'Fifty Years of Cuba's Medical Diplomacy: From Idealism to Pragmatism', *Cuban Studies*, Vol. 41, p. 85.

Folensbee, Fadhma Izri (2011). *Spreading Democracy: Supporting Dictators: Pragmatism and Ideology in US Foreign Policy in the Global War on Terror*, Saarbrucken: LAP Lambert Academic Publishing.

Ganguly, Sumit (2004). 'India's Foreign Policy Grows Up', *World Policy Journal*, Vol. 20, No. 4, pp. 44–45.

Gardini, Gian Luca and Peter Lambert (2011). *Latin American Foreign Policies: Between Ideology and Pragmatism*, New York: Palgrave Macmillan.

Godwin, Jack (2008). *The Arrow and the Olive Branch: Practical Idealism in US Foreign Policy*, Westport, CT: Praeger.

Gries, Peter Hays (2014). *The Politics of American Foreign Policy: How Ideology Divides Liberals and Conservatives Over Foreign Affairs*, Redwood City, CA: Stanford University Press.

Heilmann, Sebastian and Elizabeth J. Perry (2011). *Mao's Invisible Hand: The Political Foundations of Adaptive Governance in China*, Cambridge, MA: Harvard University Press.

Hickey, Dennis Van Vranke (2007). *Foreign Policy Making in Taiwan: From Principle to Pragmatism*, Oxon: Routledge.

Iyob, Ruth (1997). 'The Eritrean Experiment: A Cautious Pragmatism?', *Journal of Modern African Studies*, Vol. 35, No. 4, p. 667.

Jain, Rajendra K. (2011). 'From Idealism to Pragmatism: India and Asian Regional Integration', *Japanese Journal of Political Science*, Vol. 12, No. 2, pp. 227–228.

Jung, Dietrich and Wolfango Piccoli (2000). 'The Turkish-Israeli Alignment: Paranoia or Pragmatism?', *Security Dialogue*, Vol. 31, No. 1, pp. 91–104.

Khatib, Lina (2013). 'Qatar's Foreign Policy: The Limits of Pragmatism', *International Affairs*, Vol. 89, No. 2, p. 420.

Khol, Radek (2005). 'Czech Republic: Prague's Pragmatism', *Contemporary Security Policy*, Vol. 26, No. 3, pp. 470–485.

Liu Guoli (1994). *States and Markets: Comparing Japan and Russia*, Boulder, CO: Westview Press, pp. 103–104.

Maiden, Ben (1999). 'Pragmatism the Strategy for Hong Kong and China', *International Financial Law*, Vol. 18, No. 5, pp. 37–40.

McDonald, Hamish (1994). 'Mutual Benefits: A New Pragmatism Drives India's Burma Policy', *Far Eastern Economic Review*, p. 14.

Melakopides, Costas (1998). *Pragmatic Idealism Canadian Foreign Policy 1945–1995*, Montreal: McGill-Queen's University Press.

Menashri, David (2007). 'Iran's Regional Policy: Between Radicalism and Pragmatism', *Journal of International Affairs*, Vol. 60, No. 2, pp. 153–166.

Mesa-Lago, Carmelo (1978). *Cuba in the 1970s: Pragmatism and Institutionalization*, New Mexico: University of New Mexico Press.

Monshipouri, Mahmood (1998). 'Iran's Search for the New Pragmatism', *Middle East Policy*, Vol. 6, No. 2, p. 108.

Nazario, Olga (1983). *Pragmatism in Brazilian Foreign Policy: The Geisel Years, 1974–79*, Ph.D. dissertation, Ann Arbor, MI: University of Michigan.

Noorderhaven, Niels G., Jos Benders and Arjan B. Keizer (2007). 'Comprehensiveness Versus Pragmatism: Consensus at the Japanese-Dutch Interface', *Journal of Management Studies*, Vol. 44, No. 8, pp. 1349–1370.

Pye, Lucian W. (1968). *The Spirit of Chinese Politics: A Psychocultural Study of the Authority Crisis in Political Development*, Cambridge, MA: Massachusetts Institute of Technology Press.

Pye, Lucian W. (1986). 'On Chinese Pragmatism in the 1980s', *The China Quarterly*, No. 106, pp. 207–234.

Rajan, M. S. (1994). 'Pragmatism in India's Foreign Policy', *South Asian Survey*, Vol. 1, No. 1, pp. 87–89.

Ramazani, R. K. (2004). 'Ideology and Pragmatism in Iran's Foreign Policy', *Middle East Journal*, Vol. 58, No. 4, pp. 549–550.

Robinson, Linda (1994). 'Communism or Pragmatism: Fidel Castro', *US News & World Report*, Vol. 115, No. 25.

Robinson, Thomas W. (1970). 'Chou En-lai's Political Style: Comparisons with Mao Tse-Tung and Lin Piao', *Asian Survey*, Vol. 10, No. 12, pp. 1101–1116.

Rynhold, Jonathan (1996). 'China's Cautious New Pragmatism in the Middle East', *Survival: Global Politics and Strategy*, Vol. 38, No. 3, pp. 102–116.

Salvado, Francisco Romero (2003). 'Fatal Neutrality: Pragmatism or Capitulation? Spain's Foreign Policy During the Great War', *European History Quarterly*, Vol. 3, No. 3, pp. 291–315.

Schmiegelow, Henrick (1989). *Strategic Pragmatism: Japanese Lessons in the Use of Economic Theory*, New York: Praeger, p. 160.

Schreer, Benjamin (2009). 'A New "Pragmatism": Germany's NATO Policy', *International Journal*, Vol. 64, No. 2, *NATO at 60*, p. 392.

Shao Kuo-Kang (1996). *Zhou Enlai and the Foundations of Chinese Foreign Policy*, New York: St Martin's Press.

Shlapentokh, Dmitry (2011). 'Putin's Moscow Approach to Iran: Between Pragmatism and Fear', *Journal of Balkan and Near Eastern Studies*, Vol. 13, No. 2, pp. 190, 199–200, 203.

Stephens, Philip (2010). 'Cameron's Coalition Has Opted for Pragmatism', *Financial Times*.

Stoessinger, John G. (1985). *Crusaders and Pragmatists: Movers of Modern American Foreign Policy*, New York: W. W. Norton & Company.

Takeyh, Ray and Nikloas K. Gvosdev (2004). 'Pragmatism in the Midst of Iranian Turmoil', *The Washington Quarterly*, Vol. 27, No. 4, pp. 35–39.

Tan Sor-Hoon (2004). 'China's Pragmatist Experiment in Democracy: Hu Shih's Pragmatism and Dewey's Influence in China', *Metaphilosophy*, Vol. 35, No. ½, pp. 44–64.

Tsygankov, Andrei P. (2007). 'Two Faces of Putin's Great Power Pragmatism', *The Soviet and Post-Soviet Review*, Vol. 34, No. 1, pp. 104, 110.

Vassiliev, Alexei (1993). *Russian Policy in the Middle East: From Messianism to Pragmatism*, Reading: Ithaca Press.

Vihma, Antto (2011). 'India and the Global Climate Governance: Between Principles and Pragmatism', *The Journal of Environment & Development*, Vol. 20, No. 1, pp. 69–94.

Yaqub, Salim (2002). 'John Foster Dulles: Piety, Pragmatism and Power in US Foreign Policy (Review)', *Journal of Cold War Studies*, Vol. 4, No. 3, pp. 123–125.

Youde, Jeremy (2007). 'Why Look East? Zimbabwean Foreign Policy and China', *Africa Today*, Vol. 53, No. 3, pp. 3–19.

Zhao Suisheng (2004). *Chinese Foreign Policy: Pragmatism and Strategic Behaviour*, New York: M. E. Sharpe.

Note

1 Peter A. Hall and David Soskice (2001). *Varieties of Capitalism: The Institutional Foundations of Comparative Advantage*. New York: Oxford University Press.

Part II
China

7 The dao of pragmatism

Going with the flow without being swept away

Modern China's transition from a state governed according to Maoist doctrine into one driven by naked capitalism, under the banner of "socialism with Chinese characteristics" is frequently derided abroad. The change is seen as a cowardly and hypocritical betrayal of founding ideals by a cynical elite. Unsurprisingly, this is not how the evolution was perceived in China, whether by the elites or by the people. From a Chinese point of view, socialism can be summed up as the rule of the people, by the people, for the people. As such, any policy that perpetuates this situation is a good and acceptable policy. That the structure of the present Chinese political system would definitely not have met with the approval of luminaries such as Marx or Engels is unimportant: semantics is a tyranny of the majority, and if 1.4 billion Chinese citizens say that their definition is a legitimate vision of what a socialist system should be, then Marx and Engels have been roundly outvoted.

Indeed, socialism itself – however you define it – can be considered a secondary goal to that of the serene continuity of China as an entity. If ideological contortions are deemed necessary to ensure this goal, then so be it. It will certainly not be a novel situation: for over 2000 years, successive regimes employed a variety of ideological fig leaves – Confucianism, Buddhism, Daoism – for a system of government that was never anything but Legalism (rule via incentives) with Mohist (meritocratic-bureaucratic) characteristics.

Government as management

Once the true goal of the leadership – self-perpetuation – is correctly identified, then China's transition away from Maoist and Leninist principles and towards a market economy does not appear as an example of staggering hypocrisy, but rather a sensible and reasonable accommodation to circumstances. Though the terror of a party machine that had taken on a life of

DOI: 10.4324/9781003202721-9

its own and threatened to crush anyone who attempted to redirect it held the Chinese state in thrall to ideology during the middle part of the 20th century, after the first bricks fell, the edifice crumbled with startling rapidity. While a certain amount of lip service is still paid to communist theory in universities and official discourses, the day-to-day business of directing the ship of state has reverted to the ideologically neutral managerial approach that prevailed during imperial times. It is a trend that is present at all levels of government. While the system is far from perfect – as anyone who has had to deal with it in a personal capacity will attest – its flaws are the product of individual corruption and inertia, rather than dogmatism. When personal incentives do not intrude into their decision-making, officials at all levels treat their responsibilities in much the same way as managers within a business, rather than as politicians in the Western sense of the term. As we shall see over the course of the coming chapters, they tend to see their responsibility as guiding the organisations under their command through successive contingencies to achieve the best possible outcomes for all involved, rather than to embody any sort of higher principle. Indeed, for the majority, the best way that they can serve the cause of socialism with Chinese characteristics is through competent and objective management, rather than by taking up explicitly ideological positions themselves.

In agenda-setting and policy formulation, fact-based/inductive situation analysis has tended to prevail following Deng Xiaoping's accession to power. Following the motto 'seek truth from facts' (实事求是, *shi shi qiu shi*), succeeding leaders have gradually manoeuvred the state out of isolation and into the choppy waters of international engagement. Thus, Deng Xiaoping observed the change in US–Soviet relations under Reagan, and as a result settled on an 'independent' (i.e., neither US- nor Soviet-aligned) Chinese position after the normalisation of relations with the US, while nevertheless choosing to take a deliberately low-profile foreign policy line while waiting for the day that China would have the means to take a more assertive role in world affairs.[1] This 'hiding our light' (韬光养晦, *tao guang yang hui*) policy persisted throughout the Jiang Zemin years, when the Chinese leadership took a relatively self-effacing position, accepting foreign constraints in return for access to the World Trade Organisation during the post-Cold War era, when – during the 'end of history' period – free trade agreements and economic globalisation are the norm. Hu Jintao noted the strongly negative international reaction to even the slightest sign of Chinese revival when the publication of the 'peaceful rise' (中国和平崛起, *zhongguo heping jueqi*) slogan provoked disquiet among foreign observers and was rapidly changed to 'peaceful development' (中国和平发展, *zhongguo heping fazhan*) and later 'scientific development' (科学发展观, *kexue fazhan guan*). While Xi Jinping has been far more assertive in his foreign policy than any leader since Mao, the 'seek truth from facts' principle has remained a constant, being cited as frequently in his speeches and writings as in those of his predecessors.[2]

Conflicts without conflict

While China's leaders have much more power than their counterparts in many other nations, they are far from unchecked. The continued backing of their own party faction as well as the acquiescence of opposing factions is necessary to ensure the implementation of their policies. Moreover, a Chinese leader cannot generally fall back upon the possibility of stirring up a groundswell of populist support for his preferred policies if faced with dissent among his government and party colleagues. By and large, policies must be justified using expert-backed technocratic arguments, rather than sentiment or personal preferences. This tends to give an important place to foreign policy experts – Wang Huning being the representative example, having served from Jiang Zemin onwards.[3] Thus, it is only after a Chinese leader satisfies the dictates of Small-P pragmatism – and thus guarantees his own survival in the game of internal politics – that he can begin to look for Big-P pragmatic solutions to international problems.

The relatively long leadership cycles within the party also help China craft a stronger long-term grand strategy than many democratic nations with faster political turnover. This tends to give them more leeway to pursue the goals of Big-P pragmatism without being distracted by the demands of Small-P politics. While sovereignty is often put forward as a red line in Chinese foreign policy discourse, in practice, the leadership is willing to be extremely patient on the issue of territorial claims, recognising that the long-term (50–100 years) trends favour its position.[4] On the topic of the Senkaku/Diaoyu Islands, for example, both Deng and Jiang explicitly stated that they were willing to wait 100 years or more with the issue unresolved. Thus, in this case, the domestic political environment comes to favour Big-P pragmatism: in a one-party state, leaders are likely to have to live with the consequences of their decisions, meaning that making a Big-P pragmatic decision can also be a Small-P pragmatic choice. This can be observed in various ways, as the following sections will show.

Secondly, the 'whatever works' approach favoured by the Chinese leadership in addressing foreign policy often produces pragmatic policy hybrids.[5] The 'one-country-two-systems' approach to integrating Hong Kong within the mainland political system would be one example, as would the joint development of the Diaoyu Islands and South China Sea. Indeed, despite the frequent references to territorial sovereignty as a red line in official communications, successive governments have, in practice, demonstrated a remarkable willingness to find creative solutions to territorial ambiguity. While territorial disputes elsewhere in the world are a regular source of armed conflict, China's disputed claims are generally managed with comparative tolerance and willingness to accommodate short and medium-term uncertainty. How modern China was pragmatic in handling its territorial disputes (both continental and maritime) was the focus of the *Pragmatic Dragon* by Eric Hyer (2015).[6]

Often, the Chinese compromise on these issues by justifying them via the maxim 'flexible application of principles'.[7] While official policy may follow stated ideological principles, its implementation can be done in such a 'flexible' way as to effectively become the opposite of the stated intention. Thus, while the official policy is to accept no infringements of national territory, the best way to achieve this is deemed to be patience (i.e., doing very little) in the short to medium terms. Principles can be interpreted flexibly, as long as it achieves the ultimate desired policy objectives. In Chinese, this is referred to as 'dynamic application of principles to a given context' (灵活变通, *linghuo biantong*).[8]

In other words, Chinese leadership is frequently faced with the dichotomy between Small and Big-P pragmatism, as defined earlier in the introduction. They must display Small-P pragmatism internally to ensure their own survival, but this often requires an appearance of rigid adherence to ideological dogma, which is in direct contradiction with the Big-P pragmatism required in handling international relations. The result is a series of compromises of the kind described earlier, in which statements destined for internal consumption display a high degree of ideological inflexibility, but the practical measures enacted display a relatively high willingness to compromise.

The most Chinese of revolutionaries

Prof Zhang Baijia, party historian at Central Party School, made an interesting observation that Mao was the most 'Chinese' of all revolutionaries in the 1930s, which was a major factor in making him the best candidate for leader of the CCP. While many revolutionaries, such as Zhou Enlai and Deng Xiaoping, had been educated in European countries under work–study programmes, Mao had experienced only Chinese education, based around the memorisation and commenting of the classics. Mao was, for a time, an admirer of Hu Shih, who brought James Dewey from Columbia University Teachers College to teach at various institutions in Beijing, lecturing on his own ideas of pragmatism.[9] Nevertheless, Mao's first love remained the classics, despite his public endorsement of policies that denigrated the Confucianism tradition and scholarly learning more generally. Indeed, it seems probable that his adoption of communist ideology grew out of his early familiarity with Taoist dialectic. Indeed, the proximity was such that when Chiang Kai-shek was introduced to Communism, he rejected it on the basis that it had already been covered by the Chinese classics.

Coupled with Marxism's emphasis on collectivism (as opposed to individualism) and the Soviet willingness to sponsor the CCP, these factors probably explained why Marxism–Leninism took root in China amidst many other contending foreign theories.[10] Mao himself in *On Contradiction* effectively translated Marxist concepts into Chinese terms, creating a specifically Chinese vision of Communism.[11] According to this theory, when two ideas (thesis and antithesis) are in contradiction, a third (synthesis) is necessary, allowing the two contradictory concepts to co-exist and co-evolve over time. This theory has been brought to bear repeatedly in the years since – under the form of the one-country-two-systems principle, the concept of 'socialism with Chinese characteristics', for example.[12] Via ideological training in universities and party schools, the same ideas become a central part of the intellectual toolkit of the next generation of leaders.[13]

The Confucian tradition also remains a strong influence on Chinese politics, despite early Republican and Cultural-Revolution era efforts to eradicate its effect. It remains present, notably, in the high degree of respect for experts within the Chinese system, as described earlier.[14] Yet, this reverence for 'knowledge' is by and large not centred on the personality of the person who possesses it, but rather a technocratic respect for the facts themselves. One should note that the Chief of the Chinese Academy of Social Sciences is accorded Vice Premier rank of *ex-officio*, for example.

The implication of this analysis is that sociocultural factors are the main influence favouring pragmatism among the Chinese leadership and hence among the party more generally. Geography and history – notably the so-called 'century of humiliation' – does have an effect on leaders' worldviews. History and geography limit power which then constrains leaders, nevertheless, the manner of leaders' responses to these factors have primarily been dictated by their own personal leadership styles, which in turn were largely the product of sociocultural influences. These have proved an enduring structural factor with effects incorporating both ancient and modern traditions. While structural factors do not have volition as agency, sociocultural factors affect the ideational realm of both the leadership and their followers. Given that Republican institutions have been set up to effectively ensure that no other actor within the political system can challenge the party leadership when it comes to foreign policy, this makes the personal preferences of the leadership a key factor. These personal preferences are, in turn, shaped predominantly by social and cultural factors.

However, while sociocultural factors are a heavy influence, they do not necessarily exert a preponderant deterministic role. A leader may still choose to deviate from the cultural 'norm'. As history had demonstrated, pragmatism is only the guiding principle of the Chinese leadership as long as that leadership considers itself to be facing existential challenges. When a leader is strong enough to enjoy a certain amount of leeway, then ideology can become an equally or more important driving force behind policy decisions. In other words, pragmatism is not a choice when China is economically and militarily weak, but is likely to appear increasingly optional as China grows stronger.

Over the following two chapters we will look at the ways in which various leaders applied these principles, and see how they affected China's interactions with the outside world, before looking at the lessons to be drawn from China's organisational structures.

Notes

1 Interview with Zhang Yunling, 8 March 2017.
2 Xi Jinping (2014). *The Governance of China*. Beijing: Foreign Languages Press.
3 Song Haixiao (2015). *Pattern of Decision-Making of Chinese Foreign Policy* [中国外交策模式]. Guangzhou: Guangdong University of Foreign Studies: pp. 246–247.
4 Robert L. Suettinger (2003). *Beyond Tiananmen: The Politics of U.S.-China Relations 1989–2000*. Washington, DC: Brookings Institution Press: p. 420.
5 Interview with Zhao Tingyang, 20 August 2016.
6 Eric Hyer (2015). *The Pragmatic Dragon: China's Grand Strategy and Boundary Settlements*. Vancouver: UBC Press.
7 Relatedly, 'chabuduo' is a valued principle in Chinese culture which revers moderation. Interview with National University of Singapore University Professor and Chairman of East Asia Institute, Prof Wang Gungwu on 12 August 2016.
8 Interview with Zhu Chenghu, 10 March 2017. Interview with Shi Yin Hong, 29 June 2016.
9 Wang Jessica Ching-Sze (2012). *John Dewey in China: To Teach and to Learn*. New York: State University of New York Press.
10 James Bradley (2015). *The China Mirage: The Hidden History of American Disasters in Asia*. New York: Little, Brown & Co: pp. 311–312, 323.
11 Mao Zedong (1987). "On Contradiction." *Chinese Studies in Philosophy*, Vol. 19, No. 2, pp. 20–82.
12 Current strategy appears to be to engage Taiwan economically (complex interdependence), prove that 'One Country, Two Systems' can work in Hong Kong and Macau SAR, China will be so strong economically and perhaps evolve politically until one day Taiwan will yearn to return.
13 Charlotte P. Lee (2015). *Training the Party*. Cambridge: Cambridge University Press.
14 Kenneth Lieberthal and David M. Lampton (Eds.) (1992). *Bureaucracy, Politics, and Decision Making in Post-Mao China*. Washington DC: Brookings Institution Press: pp. 357–401.

8 Seeking truth from facts

不管黑猫白猫，捉到老鼠就是好猫。

(No matter if the cat is black or white, if it can catch mice then it is a good cat.)

– Sichuan proverb beloved of Deng Xiaoping

By design, China's political system of 'democratic centralism' (read: authoritarianism) makes it relatively easy for the senior leadership to implement policies, as a strong state can shorten the policy formulation–implementation loop. In fact, China's current political system can be considered a hybrid of Communism and traditional meritocratic thinking, rather than a Western-style division between political and bureaucratic actors.[1] In China, rather, the split is between party cadres and technocratic experts, though even here the lines are often blurred, with experts necessarily also being party members.[2] Thus, the differences between politicians and bureaucrats are less clear-cut in China than in the West.

Firstly, there are no popular elections *per se* for top leaders, though the Local People's Congress democratically elects grassroots leaders such as village heads.[3] Hence, with most levels of leaders appointed by either the party or the state government, the Woodrow Wilson notion of politics versus administration becomes irrelevant.[4] Secondly, the party cadre system allows the party to absorb talents from all fields into its ambit, and this includes corporate leaders, bureaucrats and even university students.[5] Individual leaders can also swing the balance one way or another. While Mao Zedong tended to prefer party loyalty over expertise, Deng Xiaoping and subsequent leaders showed a greater preference for expert advice, and Xi Jinping moved from the latter towards the former as his term in office progressed.

DOI: 10.4324/9781003202721-10

There is an extensive literature on the contrasting personalities of different Chinese leaders.[6] David Lampton, for example, traced the differing styles of leadership from Deng Xiaoping to Xi Jinping. Other relevant personalities – such as Zhu Rongji, Li Ruihuan, Zhao Qizheng and Fu Ying – have written personal autobiographies, summarising their own perspectives.

In China, the Party Chairman is very much the final arbiter of policy, though he is not always the agenda-setter and the precise way in which this is carried out can vary. Jiang Zemin and Hu Jintao, for example, were widely seen as weaker leaders, having been forced to exercise a more consensual and bureaucratic form of authority. Similarly, when a particular individual leader is not strong, the power balance tilts in favour of consensual leadership. (as Politburo Standing Committee); cases in point are Hu Jintao's more pluralistic government and who took a while to obtain military authority (Central Military Commission) from Jiang Zemin. Mao Zedong and Deng Xiaoping, by contrast, relied to a greater degree on charismatic authority. While both faced internal opposition, they tended to use political skills rather than legal–bureaucratic means to overcome it. Xi Jinping has, at various times, appeared to belong to both camps, taking a relatively low-key approach to leadership in his early years, before relying increasingly upon personality as his position grew stronger.

To get a clear perspective of how Chinese pragmatism has evolved, however, it is necessary to go back to the beginnings of modern China. We will use in-depth case studies focusing on individual leaders to demonstrate the facets and trends of the phenomenon. Through this, we intend to demonstrate that the same individual can often be pragmatic and non-pragmatic at different moments in their career, or when faced with different aspects of the policy-making process.

Mao Zedong: riding the tiger of ideology

Biographical and autobiographical literature on Mao Zedong is too vast a field to be summarised here.[7] Instead, we will focus on the specific problem of the running struggle to reconcile ideology and adaptability in Mao's leadership. Mao has frequently been written off as an ideologically motivated totalitarian by foreign observers, but a distinction should be made between the decision-making processes he adopted at different stages in his life. At the 1978 Party Congress, for example, Deng Xiaoping described the final 10 years of Mao's life – that is to say, the Cultural Revolution – as 'an aberration'.[8] Indeed, Mao's strategy during the revolution as well as his strategic writings are supremely pragmatic – it is widely recognised that his adaptability was what allowed him to prevail over the Kuomintang and his rivals within the communist party. Mao was most pragmatic in the early years in areas of party ideology and military strategy; simply put, if Mao had not been pragmatic, he would not have survived.[9] Maoism should be seen as Marxism–Leninism applied to a Chinese context in which there were more peasants than workers.[10] If Mao had adhered to a strict version of the ideology, with its primary focus on the workers, the CCP would have been unable to attract mass support.[11] Similarly, the military tactics he adopted were based around asymmetric warfare, acknowledging the CCP's limitations.[12] At the international level, while Mao himself had always preferred the prospect of a US alliance against the Japanese threat, this proved impossible given the US support for the KMT. Unable to persuade the US over to the side of the Communists, Mao settled for Soviet Union backing, tolerating their repeated attempts to meddle in internal politics in return for their financial and political support.[13]

However, a part of Mao's pragmatism had always involved the strategic use of ideology to eliminate competitors for power, notably via violent purges. As time progressed, and Mao was pushed towards 'grand old man' status within the party leadership, this tendency among the membership increasingly took on a life of its own. While this approach to stoking terror and paranoia had always been a significant component of Mao's leadership, in the early guerrilla days it had been constrained by the need to retain enough followers to fight effectively. Once his power was secured – first via his official capabilities at the top of the state, and later in his capacity as an untouchable living god – there was nothing to check the tendency. In time, as in Stalin's Russia, the paranoia created a self-fuelling state of perpetual terror, as people denounced others in a desperate attempt to prevent themselves from being denounced. Under such conditions, the pragmatism that had led the party to victory vanished, as everyone became too afraid to say anything that could potentially be used against them in a future purge. This is a theme that we will see throughout modern Chinese history, as leaders under pressure show a greater tendency to take ideological positions as a form of self-defence, taking on more pragmatic stances once the pressure is removed.

Zhou Enlai: The survivor

Zhou has been lauded as the epitome of pragmatism in modern China; indeed, there exists a book-length English-language treatment by Gao Wenqian describing Zhou's pragmatism and legacy in China's foreign policy. In it, he describes Zhou's consistent ability to let go of points deemed inessential to reach a compromise on existential matters.[14]

Zhou's pragmatism was always apparent in his domestic political activities, and particularly during the last decade of Mao's life, when the Chairman was increasingly suspicious of his staff.[15] Zhou remained Mao's deputy till his death, when many others, such as Deng Xiaoping, were purged. He showed the same adaptability in his foreign policy activities, functioning as Mao's deputy and handling much diplomatic work following the sidelining of Foreign Minister Chen Yi in the early 1960's. Zhou should be credited as the key architect of China's Five Principles of Peaceful Coexistence, which was first announced by Zhou during Sino-India talks in 1954.[16] In 1955, the same principles were reiterated and fused into the first Asian-African conference in Bandung, helping to form the nascent Non-Aligned Movement. These Five Principles remained the key foundations of the CCP's foreign relations today. Rather than taking a strongly ideological stance, the principles took a big-tent approach, emphasising 'co-existence', mutual respect, mutual non-aggression, mutual non-interference, and mutual benefit. By taking a relatively accommodating position – in contrast with strong official statements regarding the inviolability of Chinese sovereignty – Zhou's diplomatic tactics amicably resolved 14 of 20 land and maritime border disputes existing during his period of tenure.[17] Finally, Zhou played a vital role in handling the Mao–Nixon rapprochement as China's lead, interfacing with Kissinger and Nixon.

Deng Xiaoping: Making pragmatism official

Deng Xiaoping was widely regarded as Zhou Enlai's protégé, with Zhou having twice saved Deng from Mao's purges. Besides both being trained in France, it is likely that their shared preference for a pragmatic approach to politics brought them closer professionally.

While Zhou might have been the father of pragmatic Chinese diplomacy, Deng, once he acquired paramount leader status, was the key proponent of pragmatism in Chinese governance. As an individual and a charismatic party figure, Deng's pragmatism-themed slogans carried weight and had a lasting impact on the Chinese way of policy-making and implementation, both at the domestic and external levels. His key maxims on pragmatism are still used in today's China, three decades on, appealing to a strong tradition of compromise that runs through classical and modern Chinese literature, from the early Daoist rejection of idealism, to later Buddhist doctrines based on the idea that dissatisfaction with circumstances is the fault of the individual rather than the circumstances themselves.

While the slogan 'seek truth from facts' (from the *Book of Han*) was first popularised by Mao, it was Deng who used the term to connect Mao's era with his own, allowing the leadership to 'de-Mao' the party without necessarily repudiating everything that Mao had done and stood for. It has since become an article of faith among the party leadership, and notably with Xi Jinping.[18] In a similar vein, the quote used to introduce this chapter, 'no matter if the cat is black or white, if it can catch mice then it is a good cat' was a famous Dengism.[19] His fondness for the idea reflects the functionalism that dominated his time as leader, looking beyond forms and labels,[20] and focusing on the functions. This was manifested in Deng's decision to go 'independent' in foreign policy. Deng did away with China's economic and military support for fellow-socialist states, and embarked on open diplomacy with any state that was keen to engage China. Another of Deng's maxims, 'feel for stepping stones to cross the river' (摸着石头过河) reflected his preference for experimentation and the trial-and-error method. This propensity towards experimentation was most apparent in the economic modernisation effort, where Deng openly encouraged experimentation.[21] However, it was also reflected in the one-country-two-systems concept and the various special economic zones.

These differing approaches to government had a strong effect on China's relations with the rest of the world, a topic that will be covered in the next chapter.

Notes

1 Interview with Wang Yizhou, 20 July 2016.
2 Interview with Zheng Yongnian, 3 February 2017.
3 William L. Tung (2012). *The Political Institutions of Modern China*. Berlin: Springer Science & Business Media.
4 Paul P. Van Riper (1984). "The Politics-Administration Dichotomy." In *Politics and Administration: Woodrow Wilson and American Public Administration*: pp. 203–217.
5 David M. Lampton (2014). *Following the Leader: Ruling China from Deng Xiaoping to Xi Jinping*. Berkeley, CA: California University Press.
6 Li Ruihuan (2010). *Practical and Truth-Seeking* [务实求理]. Beijing: Renmin University Press. Zhu Rongji (2013). *Zhu Rongji on the Record: The Road to Reform 1991–1997*. Washington, DC: Brookings Institution Press. Zhao Qizheng (2009). *Dialogue Between Nations: Speeches by Zhao Qizheng*. Beijing: Foreign Languages Press. Wu Jianming (2006). *Foreign Policy and International Relations: Views and Analysis from Wu Jianming* [外交与国际关系: 吴建民的看法与思考]. Beijing: Renmin University Press. Fu Ying (2013). *A Voice from China: Selected Speeches of Fu Ying* [来自中国的声音: 傅莹大使演讲录]. Hong Kong: Chung Hwa Books.
7 See, for example: Mao Zedong (2007). *On Diplomacy*. Beijing: Foreign Languages Press. Xiao Shimei (2013). *Wisdom of Mao Zedong* [毛泽东智慧]. Beijing: People's Press. Zhuang Fulin (Ed.) (2010). *Thought of Mao Zedong* [毛泽东思想概论]. Beijing: Renmin University Press.
8 Xiao Shimei (2013). *Wisdom of Mao Zedong* [毛泽东智慧]. Beijing: People's Press. Translated from Zhuang Fulin (Ed.) (2010). *Thought of Mao Zedong* [毛泽东思想概论]. Beijing: Renmin University Press.
9 Interview with Ye Zhicheng, 7 March 2017.

10 Zhuang Fulin (Ed.) (2010). *Thought of Mao Zedong* [毛泽东思想概论]. Beijing: Renmin University Press: p. 15.
11 Xiao Shimei (2013). *Wisdom of Mao Zedong* [毛泽东智慧]. Beijing: People's Press: pp. 3–5. Mao Zedong (2007). *On Diplomacy.* Beijing: Foreign Languages Press: p. 216.
12 Xiao Shimei (2013). *Wisdom of Mao Zedong* [毛泽东智慧]. Beijing: People's Press: p. 80.
13 Philip Short (2016). *Mao: The Man Who Made China.* London: Bloomsbury Publishing.
14 Gao Wenqian (2007). *Zhou Enlai: The Last Perfect Revolutionary.* New York: Public Affairs. Hu Zhangming (2015). *Wisdom of Zhou Enlai: Why the Famous Became Famous* [大智周恩来：伟人何以成为伟人]. Beijing: Guangming Daily Press.
15 Gao Wenqian (2007). *Zhou Enlai: The Last Perfect Revolutionary.* New York: Public Affairs.
16 The Five Principles are: (1) Mutual respect for each other's territorial integrity and sovereignty; (2) Mutual non-aggression; (3) Mutual non-interference in each other's internal affairs; (4) Equality and cooperation for mutual benefit; (5) Peaceful co-existence. Mao (2007): p. 127.
17 Chung Chien-peng (2004). *Domestic Politics, International Bargaining and China's Territorial Disputes.* New York: Routledge.
18 Xi Jinping (2014). *The Governance of China.* Beijing: Foreign Languages Press.
19 Interview with Jin Canrong, 25 December 2016.
20 Interview with Ezra Vogel, 17 May 2017.
21 Zhang Wei-Wei (1996). *Ideology and Economic Reform Under Deng Xiaoping, 1978–1993.* London: Routledge.

9 Red lines (and pink lines) in Chinese foreign policy

As with the tradition from socialism to socialism with Chinese characteristics described earlier, Chinese diplomacy since the founding of the republic has often been based around the taking of uncompromising ideological positions on red-line issues, and then demonstrating almost infinite flexibility in their application. So, while China may refuse to give way on symbolic matters such as the Senkaku/Diaoyu Islands, the nine-dash line and Taiwan, the leadership has also repeatedly stated that it is willing to wait almost indefinitely to see these issues resolved. Thus, when Mao Zedong met Henry Kissinger and enjoyed the following exchange:

Chairman Mao:	'But you now have the Taiwan of China.'
Secretary Kissinger:	'But we will settle that between us.'
Chairman Mao:	'In a hundred years.'
Secretary Kissinger:	'That's what the Chairman said the last time I was here.'
Chairman Mao:	'Exactly.'
Secretary Kissinger:	'It won't take a hundred years. Much less.'
Chairman Mao:	'It's better for it to be in your hands. And if you were to send it back to me now, I would not want it, because it's not wantable. There are a huge bunch of counter-revolutionaries there. A hundred years hence we will want it (gesturing with his hand), and we are going to fight for it.'

In this chapter, we intend to look in much closer detail at two specific historical episodes, to examine carefully how China's idiosyncratic mixture of principles and pragmatism affects its relations with the rest of the world.

DOI: 10.4324/9781003202721-11

The Nixon–Mao rapprochement

While the rapprochement between the US and China under Richard Nixon and Mao Zedong is regularly brought up as an example of American foreign policy pragmatism, the final outcome also required no small amount of compromise on the Chinese side – with compromise being the key *via postiva* indicator of a pragmatic approach, as described in the introduction earlier. While Nixon started his Presidency with an intent to move closer to China and use that proximity as a lever against the Soviet Union, these plans would have remained mere plans if Mao was not receptive to the idea. Detailed accounts of the episode exist, written by both the Chinese and the American side, making it a particularly useful example to begin with.

The US insistence on preserving its relationship with the Kuomintang (KMT) even following its retreat to Taiwan and the communist domination of the Chinese mainland has reinforced the ideological split between the two governments. This was deepened further by the intervention of the People's Volunteer Army on the side of the Korean People's Army in the Korean War. Despite the Chinese government's decision to frame the action as a spontaneous popular uprising in an effort to avoid entering into an official state of war with the US, the public on both the US and the Chinese sides were well aware of the nature of the enemy that their troops – both volunteers and conscripts – were fighting against. The context was thus defined by both parties as an ideological one, making it difficult for them to subsequently reverse their positions or reach a compromise – the key indicator of pragmatic decision-making as described earlier.

The result was that, even as a closer relationship began to seem like an advisable strategic choice for both sides, the prospect was hampered by the risk of any attempt at rapprochement being perceived as a humiliating climb-down by the enemy, domestic public opinion, and the international community in general. It was in the US's interests to draw down the conflict in Vietnam and acquire a bulwark against the USSR in the East, just as it was in China's interests to gain support in its increasingly fractious relationship with the Soviets. Nevertheless, for many years, ideological and prestige reasons have made any move on either side a highly risky proposition.

Throughout the years leading up to the deal, Mao had become increasingly open to the idea of a rapprochement with the United States as a way to bolster the positions of both nations against the Soviet Union, which had gradually become a common enemy. Mao eventually tasked his officials with reconsidering China's strategic situation – the policy formulation stage of the process. Unsurprisingly, the committee recommended that China embark on a strategic alliance with the US. Foreign Minister Chen Yi had, in fact, been advocating for a US alliance since the early 1960's, when the first signs of a Sino-Soviet spilt appeared (fact-based analysis after ground reality had changed and Chen Yi was recommending a policy-reversal), though his loyalty to Mao had then been called into question, leading to him being politically side-lined. This episode is an example of Mao behaving non-pragmatically – focusing on his wish to become a leader of the third-world movement, rather than "seeking truth from facts" – the fact demonstrates the ways in which ideological agenda-setting can have the power to restrict policy formulation and implementation, preventing reliance upon objective cost–benefit analyses and thus limiting strategic thinking. The fact that such a possibility could subsequently be considered shows the weakening of the ideological pressure under the force of circumstances, allowing greater room for compromise. The main trigger for Mao's new willingness to consider a policy reversal was the Sino-Soviet border skirmishes in 1969, but Mao had also paid close attention to the Soviet invasion of Czechoslovakia in 1968. With a growing perception of vulnerability to the Soviet threat, any remaining sense of loyalty to a fellow socialist power waned quickly. When Nixon made the first move via Pakistani diplomatic channels, Mao responded positively.

The Shanghai Communiqué issued in 1972 marked a complete policy reversal, a U-turn on the anti-US line held since the Korean war. Nevertheless, in scrutinising the communiqué, one may observe a relatively high degree of strategic ambiguity at play. The long preamble of the communiqué articulating the fact that both the US and China are still at odds with each other over ideology is significant.[1] This preamble was necessary to persuade domestic audiences in both the US and China that both governments were determined to remain true to their ideology, and the goal of the new agreement was not for either side to repudiate its principles, but rather to come together despite their differences to fight a greater evil. In order for the Communiqué to succeed domestically, this preamble was necessary. Similarly, the Communiqué was careful to state that both the US and China would continue to define the status of Taiwan according to their own terms. These demonstrate both sides' willingness to compromise and flexibility in implementation to ensure the Communiqué will pass both countries' domestic audience tests.

While everything was done to reduce the risks that the Communiqué would be seen as such, the fact remains that it was a significant ideological compromise – not to mention a pride-swallowing exercise – for both sides. In other words, a direction set during the agenda-setting stage, was reversed at the policy-formulation and implementation stages. It is noteworthy that during this period, Mao was still championing the idea of socialist brotherhood abroad, and providing support to other socialist states, such as Angola.[2] Nevertheless, on matters perceived to be of existential urgency, this belief in cross-national loyalty to a shared socialist cause could happily be dropped in favour of a more immediately pragmatic stance.

Nevertheless, the risks inherent in abandoning a stance based upon ideological principles in favour of one recommended by circumstances were such that they could only be taken by leaders benefiting from a certain amount of room for manoeuvre at home. While the Nixon-Mao rapprochement was a significant step, domestic disturbances and weak leadership in both countries effectively prevented any follow-up for some years afterwards. On the Chinese side, in particular, anyone suggesting deviating radically from accepted doctrine for reasons of expedience would have been risked not only his job, but his life immediately following Mao's death. Policy stalled for some time during the aftermath of the Watergate scandal and during the Gang of Four/Hua Guofeng years, for domestic rather than international reasons. Nevertheless, the external factors pushing for closer cooperation did not disappear, and when leaders with more latitude to act – Jimmy Carter on the US side and Deng Xiaoping in China – came to power, the prospects for further compromise brightened.

The Carter–Deng normalisation

Though the Nixon–Mao negotiations had been underpinned by the need of both sides to appear to maintain the ideological positions set out during the agenda-setting stage, in reality they marked a significant reversal/compromise. This compromise, once assimilated into the mindsets of policymakers, could then effectively set the agenda for future talks.

While the Nixon–Mao accord set the stage for normalisation, the process was only completed under Jimmy Carter and Deng Xiaoping, via negotiations taking place in 1978–79. The reasons for the delay were primarily domestic.[3] Nixon had been hampered in his quest for normalisation due to the Watergate scandal. While Kissinger was not implicated the scandal and continued to serve as Secretary of State under Gerald Ford, progress was then limited by Chinese domestic political struggles, while Ford was also domestically weak due to the post-Watergate distrust in the executive. On the Chinese side, Mao was increasingly ill, as was Premier Zhou Enlai, who was Mao's de-facto deputy and wielded a high degree of influence in foreign policy matters. The power-struggle that followed Mao and Zhou's decline and death was protracted and disruptive to regular policy-making. For the leaders of the time, ensuring their own survival by emphasising loyalty to party ideology predominated over any concerns about the national interest, and dominated the agenda-setting stage of any policy-making. Relations with the US were simply less important than day-to-day survival in the hothouse atmosphere of paranoia that prevailed. This is the first significant example of the pendulum swinging in the opposite direction: when Mao had felt more secure in his power (prior to the Great Leap Forward and the Cultural Revolution), he was able to act more pragmatically. Now that domestically weaker leaders were fighting for control, none benefited from the room for manoeuvre necessary to exercise pragmatic diplomatic strategies. Once again, we see ideology predominating at the agenda-setting stage of the policy process.[4]

Emphasising the pressure to be ideologically correct that prevailed during this period, Deng was essentially side-lined for a third time. It was only after Mao's death that Deng was gradually 'rescued' by his lieutenants and made his way back to the political centre stage. The result was that almost ten years passed before the normalisation process could be restarted, after Deng grew strong enough internally to be able to impose his own line upon the Party. In 1981, Deng replaced the official leader, Hua Guofeng, with a protégé of his own, Hu Yaobang, and was – from that point on – equipped to take a far more assertive position, and begin setting the agenda according to his own personal preferences, which leaned towards pragmatic cost–benefit analysis and policy experimentation, rather than dogma.[5]

This time, closer relations with the US were dictated – on the Chinese side, at least – not by military imperatives, but by economic ones. To be fully effective, Deng's economic policies required access to international export markets. This, in turn, required the normalisation of relations with the US. Once again, it was necessary to sacrifice principles for gains, conducting a policy reversal compromise, whether the environment was propitious for resetting the agenda or not. On the US side, at this point, enthusiasm for closer relations with China was minimal. Jimmy Carter favoured the alliance with Taiwan, and did not wish to risk the progress made with the Soviet Union on the Strategic Arms Limitation Treaty (SALT) by appearing to favour China. Moreover, there was additional pressure from the US public, which was shown by polls to strongly support the alliance with Taiwan.[6]

The result was that China entered the new round of negotiations in a comparatively weak position – something that the negotiators would have been well aware would increase the likelihood of needing to compromise on previous positions. While they required a good outcome for Deng's economic reform to realise its full potential, the US side was more than a little ambivalent regarding the prospect of a closer relationship with the People's Republic of China (PRC). The result was that Deng was obliged to take a pragmatic view with regard to Taiwan during the negotiation process, distinguishing the national position (that Taiwan was an integral part of China's territory) and the national Strategy (that any military assertion of this claim could wait). Moreover, Deng showed more willingness to compromise on language than Mao, dropping Mao's insistence on the 'liberation of Taiwan' in official documents and favouring a softer and more feasible vision of the reunification of Taiwan in the long term. By this point, the practical compromises/reversals made in previous exchanges had become a part of the negotiators' and the public's mindsets to a sufficient degree to set the agenda for subsequent negotiations.

This willingness to back-peddle slightly on the Taiwan issue, allowed the US side to sell the final agreement to its own domestic audience as a "win–win deal", arguing that it had helped to ensure stability in Asia without jeopardising the SALT accord or – technically, at least – compromising its position on the defence of Taiwan. In fact, Carter had also demonstrated willingness to compromise by not writing into the agreement an explicit declaration that the US would protect Taiwan with force if necessary. This decision received some domestic criticism, but most observers agreed that this semantic sleight of hand had been necessary to conclude a successful agreement.

Not for the first time, the Chinese leadership has taken the pragmatic decision to violate one of its own "red lines", because doing so seems more advantageous than refraining from it. As before, this was done at the policy formulation/implementation stage, rather than during the agenda-setting stage, with the aim of reconciling Small-P and Big-P pragmatism. It is interesting to note that the same era also saw the initial development of the 'one-country-two-systems' concept. Originally mooted as a potential solution to the Taiwan problem, the concept was later applied to the Hong Kong and Macau Special Administrative Regions. The concept was a useful one for the Chinese authorities, in that it appeared to give every party what they wanted, while still allowing enough ambiguity for power politics to play a role as the situation developed in the future and Chinese influence grew stronger. In other words, the Chinese side was willing to grant any number of concessions to ensure formal recognition of its territorial claims, safe in the knowledge that, in the long term, it would be able to use its political strength to gain real authority over the areas in question.

Deng was also willing to sacrifice principles at the international level to help ensure the success of the domestic economy, via the Four Modernisations Policy. This policy should effectively be regarded as the cornerstone of Deng's international grand strategy, despite its domestic focus. Deng was thus willing to compromise and lean towards the US for military and civilian technological transfer. Similarly, he walked back Mao's focus on military supremacy, freezing the military upgrade budget in order to fund economic modernisation. Deng essentially eliminated China's special relationships with Socialist countries, in order to secure friendly relations with all states. This was particularly clear in Southeast Asia, where Deng ceased propaganda efforts in an attempt to mend ties, while inviting overseas Chinese businessmen to invest in the mainland.

As these two cases show, Chinese pragmatism is strongly influenced in its application by the personal style of the leader at the time, and perhaps even more so by his domestic position, and perhaps even more so by his domestic position, which often requires trade-offs between Small-P and Big-P pragmatism. A strong leader has greater scope to go against – or even to rewrite – matters of ideological principles. While doing so remains a risk, he is more likely to judge himself as able to weather any adverse consequences if the potential prize is large enough. By contrast, a weaker politician is more likely to be driven by loss-aversion to adopt a strategy likely to annoy the least possible number of people.

Chinese pragmatism as a two-level game

The authoritarian system in China tends to produce analyses that focus on the personalities of the leaders when analysing decisions. However, as the present chapter demonstrates, these leaders do not operate unchecked, and can be seen to consistently moderate their personal preferences to accommodate the structural forces to which they are subjected to.

In situations of domestic uncertainty, we have seen, there is a tendency to descend into a purity spiral, whereby every individual is obliged to constantly protest extreme devotion to the group ideology, for fear of being denounced and purged. By contrast, when outside pressures may come to the fore, there is greater pressure to compromise on ideology – something that can nevertheless only happen when the leader in question is powerful enough domestically to ensure that his decisions will be accepted, even in the event that they seem to contradict fundamental ideological principles.[7]

Thus, despite not being subject to the conventional democratic constraints that may operate elsewhere, Chinese leaders can be seen to be functioning in a two-level game situation, wherein they must reconcile domestic and international win-sets. While pragmatism may be advantageous abroad, it only becomes feasible when a leader is strong enough domestically to withstand the political ramifications of his ideological compromises.

In this chapter, we have shown how pragmatism is interpreted in the Chinese context, as well as the ways in which individual leaders have moved between non-pragmatic and pragmatic positions as a result of the internal and external pressures to which they are subject in the policy-making process. Each individual leader has been shown to move between Small-P pragmatism and Big-P pragmatism as a function of the pressures applied, being Small-P pragmatic when faced with internal threats to their own survival, but often demonstrating Big-P pragmatism on the international stage when allowed the internal leeway to do so.

Notes

1 Hosted on the State Department website, Accessed from: https://photos. state.gov/libraries/ait-taiwan/171414/ait-pages/shanghai_e.pdf. Accessed on 25 July 2019.
2 Roderick MacFarquhar (Ed.) (1993). *The Politics of China, 1949–1989.* Cambridge: Cambridge University Press.
3 William C. Kirby et al. (2006). *The Normalization of US-China Relations: An International History.* Cambridge, MA: Harvard University Press.
4 Interview with Chas Freeman, 1 June and 25 July 2017.
5 Lu Ning (2018). *The Dynamics of Foreign-Policy Decision Making in China.* New York: Routledge.
6 Garrison, Jean A. (2002). "Explaining Change in the Carter Administration's China Policy: Foreign Policy Adviser Manipulation of the Policy Agenda." *Asian Affairs: An American Review*, Vol. 29, No. 2, pp. 83–98.
7 Interview with Shi Yin Hong, 29 June 2016.

Part III
Singapore

10 The ideology of pragmatism

'We were in no position to be fussy about high-minded principles. We had to make a living.'

– Lee Kuan Yew

In contrast with the Chinese case described earlier, wherein overt ideology tends to predominate at the agenda-setting stage and pragmatism in implementation, in the Singapore case, the agenda-setting stage is often characterised by active insistence on Big-P pragmatism, while implementation risks getting bogged down in Small-P pragmatism or even ideology. In the present chapter, we explain why and how this happens.

Singapore celebrated surviving its first 50 years as an independent state in 2015.[1] In the years since it shot 'from the third world to the first', becoming an Asian tiger despite an almost total lack of natural resources, Singapore's success has been credited variously to luck, meritocracy and pragmatism, among other factors.[2]

Indeed, Singapore's explosive success seems to have surprised its own residents as much as anyone else, and a great deal of ink has been spilled by academics and memoirists alike, attempting to work out how exactly it arrived at its present situation. While the pragmatism of the first generation of leaders under Lee Kuan Yew is invariably given high billing, the precise connotations of the term vary sharply from author to author. Among former politicians and civil servants, the tone tends to be one of admiration (or self-congratulation), in autobiographical texts brimming with pride at having avoided the pitfalls of ideology that engulfed so many neighbouring states, and treasuring instead a Swiss-style neutrality and willingness to do business with any partner. The same has tended to be true for the authors of popular treatments of the topic, aimed mainly at foreign readers wishing to understand the Asian tiger economies. On the other hand, local academics have tended to be much more sceptical about the concept, often seeing

DOI: 10.4324/9781003202721-13

in the pragmatism of the first generation of leaders a grasping peasant cynicism at best, and an excuse for vicious and profoundly unjust crackdowns on political opponents at worst. So who is right?

In this chapter, we will take a look at what pragmatism means in the practical, everyday context of Singapore politics and administration, before going on in subsequent chapters to look at its effects on Singapore's foreign policy, before trying to draw all the threads together and coming up with a set of unifying principles that describe and define Singapore pragmatism, as distinct from other countries' approaches. The goal is to demonstrate that, in contrast with the China case, an apparent devotion to Big-P pragmatism, as defined in the introduction, can gradually be elided into a devotion merely to its outward appearances, driven by the constraints of Small-P pragmatism. Under such circumstances, the Small-P imperative of performing pragmatism can potentially come to crowd out the ability to evaluate and respond to the needs of Big-P pragmatism and Strategic Pragmatism.

Experimentation and arguments

While the precise ethical and political implications of the Singapore leadership's dedication to pragmatism are up for debate, its effects on the ground are relatively clear.

In practice, it translates into a policy-making system geared towards facts-based strategic analysis of the situation, scenario planning with regard to the various possibilities, checklist-based decision-making and flexibility at the tactical, operational and strategic levels.

During the agenda-setting and policy formulation phases of the policy process, Singapore leaders use a fact-based or inductive analysis of situation. This was originally seen as the fundamental 'added value' contributed by the governmental elites.[3] This could also include revising existing policies if they proved unsuccessful or unpopular. One obvious example would be the case of the hugely unpopular graduate mothers scheme (an openly eugenics-based policy that provided incentives for women with university degrees to have more children). Though the majority of the government supported the policy, they nevertheless accepted that the electoral price to be paid for its introduction – a 12.8% swing to the opposition – was a sign that they had underestimated the strength of public sentiment on the issue. As Goh Chok Tong put it: 'It was not sustainable. By then even those of us who were in favour of it knew the political costs. It may cost us to lose the election. That was the time when we began to modify. We were all pragmatists on what was doable and what was not.'[4] While Lee Kuan Yew's authoritarian treatment of internal opponents who were unwilling to allow themselves to be co-opted into the PAP system is well known, he nevertheless remained open to argument on the part of those whose systemic loyalty was not under question, as a good means to both elucidate facts and develop better strategies. As Bilahari Kausikan puts it: 'Mr. Lee suffered no fools. He often tried to intimidate you into agreement. But this is not the same thing as being intolerant. . . . Even when he did not agree, he listened. He never thought that he had all the answers. He never hesitated to change his mind if the situation warranted it.'[5] Cabinet meetings were never content to simply rubber-stamp Lee's decisions.[6] It was recorded that Lee and Goh often quarrelled over policy positions, and Lee would relent if Goh's logic was sufficiently persuasive. After his retirement from Prime Ministership (as Senior Minister and later Minister Mentor), Lee continued to devote himself to surveying and analysing changes in the international situation and recommended policy changes via the Cabinet accordingly. It can be considered an endorsement of his fact-based adaptability that Senior Lee's views remained sought-after (and thus apparently considered uncontroversial enough to be palatable) by the international community as an elder world statesman, by both capitalist and socialist states, democratic and authoritarian governments.[7]

The same tendency can be observed in Goh Keng Swee's preference for immediate, fact-based analysis, and personal verification of facts.[8] As defence minister, Goh was famous for uninformed spot-checks: Goh would fly in by helicopter or car, unannounced, to observe the 'unrehearsed' aspect of military life.

Similarly, Goh's 'fact-based' pragmatism can be seen in his decision to experiment with 'export-oriented growth' when the rest of the developing world favoured import-substitution. Goh surveyed the economic development models of the world and was not convinced that import-substitution model would work for Singapore as our domestic market was too small and we lack natural resources'.[9] Hence, the geography of Singapore (size, demographics, lack of natural resources) compelled policymakers to think of alternatives to the widely-accepted panacea that was import-substitution at the time. Thus, Singapore experimented with alternative models, which soon averred themselves appropriate to the city-state's situation, but nevertheless avoided being lulled into complacency by this short-term success, with the Economic Development Board (EDB) continuing to tweak and update policy as Singapore's economic situation evolved. The EDB's willingness to drop heretofore successful strategies when circumstances indicated that an alternative approach was likely to yield even better results was well-documented by Edgar Schein (1996).[10] Thus, despite the EDB's resounding success in helping the country develop, the government took pains to avoid complacency and the accretion of red tape, subjecting the organisation to continual policy upgrades, including a root-and-branch reform in the 1980s. Even personnel who had played crucial roles in creating the economic prosperity enjoyed in Singapore at that point were moved to other departments if it was felt that their skills were no longer adapted to dealing with an economy that was now increasingly focused on higher value added goods and services. Chairman Philip Yeo described the change thus: 'Because economic development is dynamic, we have to continually maintain and improve Singapore's competitive advantage.'[11] The idea that to stay in place is to fall behind is one that has become increasingly commonplace in Singapore as it has developed. Where pragmatic policies were originally justified by an urgent need to catch up to the rest of the developed world, they are now justified by the equally urgent need to stay ahead of the rapidly industrialising nations of East Asia. As PM Lee Hsien Loong puts it: 'It is really a tidal wave, a tsunami coming in our direction and the only way to get out of the trouble is to rise above the tsunami by training ourselves, developing expertise and doing things which they cannot do yet in China but which we can do now in Singapore so that we can make a living for ourselves in order to improve our lives.'[12]

However, pragmatism, *per* the Singaporean vision of the concept, does not mean a complete reliance upon short-term expediency. In fact, during policy formulation, Singapore prides itself on long-term scenario-planning and future thinking. Once again, this is a reflection of Lee Kuan Yew's own vision of the role of a leader: 'My job is to be a long-range radar, to look ahead and then share with the government and give them my advice.'[13] Scenario-planning was imported from Shell Petroleum and actively practised in various ministries (with the author being actively involved in the practice and teaching of the method). Diverse scenario-planning methodologies (e.g., 'future forward' and 'future backward'), which are now widely available in open source literature, were also used. Former Civil Service Head, Peter Ho, was a firm believer in these methods and established the Centre for Strategic Futures in 2009, reporting directly to the Prime Minister's Office. Various ministries now have dedicated staff responsible for 'future' work. Where future methodologies attempt to anticipate new complexity and unexpected events, scenario-planning takes a linear, goal-oriented approach.[14] A practical example of this long-term planning can be found in Singapore's urban planning system. Urban planners have three types of plans: concept plan, master plan and development guide plans. Concept plans are 30–40 year plans, while master plans seek to operationalise and adjust concept plans in shorter time periods of 5–10 years. Singapore is divided into 55 planning areas and future development plans are prepared by Urban Redevelopment Authority as development guide plans to systematically and transparently communicate to the private sector.[15] For example, the 1971 Concept Plan sets out the development needs of projected population of four million by 1992. Similarly, the 1991 Concept Plan incorporated 55 Development Guide Plans, which in turn fed into the 1998 Master Plan.

During policy formulation, Singapore's ideology of pragmatism led it to favour policy hybrids, and thus innovation. The solution selected for a particular problem was often not a part of one or another theoretical or ideological system, but a hybrid. For example, while the People's Action Party was initially influenced by pro-collective/egalitarian aims of Fabian socialism, it was realised that a full-scale welfare state would bankrupt the state and hence a hybrid system was preferred: a capitalist economy with income redistribution in housing, education and healthcare. While the PAP's exact positioning on the left–right continuum has differed over time, its fondness for the idea of a hybrid model has remained constant since 1965.[16]

Singapore has also made concerted efforts to institutionalise pragmatic decision-making. As mentioned earlier, the debate process in Pre-Cabinet and Cabinet meetings aims to ensure that the blind spots and feasibility of proposed policies are actively addressed by ministers who have helmed similar ministerial portfolios before.[17] The logic and common sense of a policy will always be analysed to ensure soundness and coherence. Resource availability is a key criterion, given that Singapore is a small state with limited resources. Policies that require too many resources and where the costs outweigh the benefits will not be approved. This resource availability check ensures policy design is 'implementable' within Singapore's abilities. Lastly, there is a check on systemic effects to ensure policies do not bring short-term benefits at the expense of long-term costs.[18]

Lastly, during the policy implementation phase, Singapore's small state and government enables the government to ensure that feedback loops are tight. The close relationship between politicians and civil servants means that during implementation, the feedback loop back from implementers to decision-makers is short for tactical adjustments, operational changes and even policy reversals to be made. For example, when G7 expanded to G20, there was an apprehension that the economic interests of smaller states could be crowded out. They were able to feed the information back to HQ quickly, and work with HQ to spearhead the Forum of Small States (FOSS) at United Nations to aggregate voices of smaller states.[19] While feedback loops and decisions on policy reversals tend to be internal to government and little-publicised, Lee Kuan Yew acknowledged (for example) that the 'stop at two' birth-control policy had been too successful, leading to a collapse in birth rates and a growing demographic time bomb. Referring to criticism that it had been wrong, Mr Lee wrote: "Yes and no." Without lower population growth, unemployment and schooling problems would not have been solved, he argued. "But we should have foreseen that the better-educated would have two or fewer children, and the less-educated four or more." In hindsight, "we would have refined and targeted our campaign differently" right from the 1960s, he said. In recent years, the government poured money and effort into trying to get Singaporeans to have more babies, but the low birth rate has persisted. "I cannot solve the problem and I have given up," he said, "leaving the task to the new generation of leaders."[20]

Examples from domestic politics give a useful impression of the thought processes – both individual and collective – that go into making policy, but internal politics can also be an imperfect Petri dish for analysing choices. Given the absence of counterfactuals, the temptation to make post hoc judgments can be almost insurmountable. By contrast, international politics offers a suite of comparators, insofar as any given situation can be analysed via the differing reactions of the states responding to it. In such a way, it effectively becomes possible to situate their respective policies on a continuum, from highly ideological to entirely pragmatic. In the following chapter, we will take a look at Singapore's foreign policy choices since independence, comparing them with those made by its neighbours, partners and adversaries.

Notes

1 Kwa Chong Guan, Derek Thiam Soon Heng and Tai Yong Tan (2009). *Singapore, a 700-Year History: From Early Emporium to World City*. Singapore: National Archives of Singapore.
2 Prashanth Parameswaran (2015). "10 Lessons from Lee Kuan Yew's Singapore." *The Diplomat*, 24 March 2015. Accessed from: https://thediplomat.com/2015/03/10-lessons-from-singapores-success/. Accessed on 1 January 2019.
3 Ng Kok Song (2015). *Up Close with Lee Kuan Yew: Insights from Colleagues and Friends*. Singapore: Marshall Cavendish: p. 153.
4 Peh Shing Huei (2019). *Tall Order: The Goh Chok Tong Story*. Singapore: World Scientific Publishing Company Pte. Limited: p. 157.
5 Bilahari Kausikan (2015). *Up Close with Lee Kuan Yew: Insights from Colleagues and Friends*. Singapore: Marshall Cavendish: p. 160.
6 Interview with Suppiah Dhanabalan, 17 January 2018.
7 Graham Allison, Robert D. Blackwill, Ali Wyne and Henry A. Kissinger (2013). *Lee Kuan Yew: The Grand Master's Insights on China, the United States, and the World*. Cambridge, MA: Massachusetts Institute of Technology Press: pp. XIII–XXIII.
8 Interview with Wang Gungwu, 12 August 2016.
9 Interview with Suppiah Dhanabalan, 17 January 2018.
10 Edgar C. Schein (1996). *Strategic Pragmatism: The Culture of Singapore's Economic Development Board*. Cambridge, MA: Massachusetts Institute of Technology Press: pp. 99–101.

11 Edgar C. Schein (1996). *Strategic Pragmatism: The Culture of Singapore's Economic Development Board*. Cambridge, MA: Massachusetts Institute of Technology Press: pp. 99–101.

12 Lee Hsien Loong, National Day Rally Speech, PMO, 14 August 2011. Accessed from: www.pmo.gov.sg/Newsroom/prime-minister-lee-hsien-loongs-national-day-rally-2011-speech-english. Accessed on 4 May 2019.

13 Ng Kok Song (2015). *Up Close with Lee Kuan Yew: Insights from Colleagues and Friends*. Singapore: Marshall Cavendish: p. 153.

14 Lecture by Peter Ho, "Scenario Planning and Horizon Scanning," 5 September 2013.

15 Centre for Liveable Cities (2016). "Urban Development: From Urban Squalor to Global City." In *Urban Systems Studies*. Singapore: Centre for Liveable Cities: pp. 16, 81–82, 86–87.

16 Neo Boon Siong and Geraldine Chen (2007). *Dynamic Governance: Embedding Culture, Capabilities and Change in Singapore*. Singapore: World Scientific: pp. 166–177.

17 Yasmine Yahya (2018). "Lim Hng Kiang: Longest-Serving MTI Minister Who Prefers Talking Trade to Getting Personal." *Straits Times*, 27 April 2018.

18 Interview with Suppiah Dhanabalan, 17 January 2018.

19 Tommy Koh and Chang Li Lin (2009). *The Little Red Dot: Reflections by Singapore's Diplomats, Vol. II*. Singapore: World Scientific.

20 *Today Online* (2015). "Policies for the Bedroom and Beyond," 23 March 2015. Accessed from: www.todayonline.com/rememberinglky/policies-bedroom-and-beyond. Accessed on 31 March 2019.

11 A friend to everybody and an ally to none

Running the United States is like being in command of an aircraft carrier. You will not capsize. Steering a small and young country is more like shooting rapids in a canoe.

– Goh Chok Tong

While Singapore's determination to take the most advantageous aspects of socialist and capitalist systems while committing to neither is a valuable lesson for any student of state pragmatism, it was in the field of foreign relations that the leadership tended to feel the most vulnerable, and thus to focus most intently on pure survival. As described in the previous chapter, from the beginning, there existed a sense that principles were a luxury that a small, poor state simply could not afford. Interestingly, however, this sentiment has survived despite the evaporation of the principal threats – from Indonesia and communist groups in Southeast Asia. While Singapore's wealth has bought it power beyond its weight in the region, and the security threats that hung over it in the past are a distant memory, there remains a strong tendency in the government to view all politics in terms of total war, in which the slightest slip or indulgence could be fatal.

In this chapter, we will look in detail at some examples of Singapore foreign policy decision-making episodes, in which sentiment was consistently sacrificed on the altar of practical gain. It is interesting to contrast this with the Chinese position described earlier, wherein the government takes a flexible position in practice while making much noise about the inviolability of its principled positions.

Pragmatism in foreign policy has generally been less controversial than in domestic policy. In foreign policy, the continual presence of outside threats can be used to justify pragmatic decision-making. In domestic policy, this 'external threat' justification has grown less persuasive in recent years, with the decline of the communist threat. The danger of pragmatism in foreign

DOI: 10.4324/9781003202721-14

policy, however, is that external actors may be antagonised by the lack of policy consistency across time. For example, Singapore has thus far applied a pragmatic principle of duality to engage both the US and China, but any misstep risks being regarded as 'two-timing' both powers. Singapore has managed to embrace duality thus far because it is too small to be a threat and it has managed to demonstrate its utility to both powers. As China grows stronger and more assertive in regional issues, however, this line is likely to become increasingly difficult to walk, and Singapore may eventually find itself obliged – in the name of pragmatism – to pick a side. In doing so, however, it will be crucial for politicians and bureaucrats to avoid the temptation to perform pragmatism rather than applying it. The elevation of the concept to a panacea is liable to make it tempting for politicians to use it as a justification for whatever policies appeal to them, rather than to put in the hard work of actually trying to develop policies on a pragmatic basis. Thus Big-P pragmatism can tend to decline into Small-P pragmatism, producing diminishing returns over time, a tendency which – as we shall show – Singapore in particular should beware of this tendency.

Bombs and flowers: The konfrontasi era

Indonesia, under President Sukarno, launched attacks on Singapore and Malaysia as part of a reunification plan for Greater Indonesia. Indonesian special forces landed in Singapore and attacked the MacDonald House. This 'konfrontasi' policy contributed partially to the formation of what eventually became the Association for Southeast Asian Nations (ASEAN), as a community established by five countries (Malaysia, Singapore, Indonesia, the Philippines and Brunei) to check the errant behaviour of a regional hegemon (Indonesia). In this case, therefore, the agenda had already been set in ideological terms by the Indonesian side, and the Singapore government was forced to find a way to deal with the situation. Lee Kuan Yew had always been apprehensive of Indonesia because of its size. However, he also accepted that that Indonesian neighbour is too close and too big to risk open conflict. As a result, Lee Kuan Yew focused on engaging in Indonesia to ensure Singapore's survival. Lee Khoon Choy was tasked with improving Indonesia–Singapore relations as Singapore's Ambassador to Indonesia. During Lee Kuan Yew's introductory visit to Indonesia, he scattered petals at the grave of the Special Forces soldiers that had participated in the attack on Singapore. This act was well-received by Indonesians and was not considered to imply a loss of face domestically in the same way that leaving a wreath may have done. This symbolic act enabled the two nations to put past feuds behind them and focus on establishing better relations.[1]

Where a more overtly nationalistic leader would likely have refused to make such a conciliatory gesture, the Singaporean leadership apparently decided that any loss of face would be more than compensated by the resulting economic and security gains that a warmer relationship would bring.

Unlinking from Malaysia

Singapore's separation from Malaysia in the 1960s created tension and awkwardness for both parties. While much attention was given to the diplomatic manoeuvring between the two states, the separation also implied a great deal of smaller infrastructure-related problems. For example, after the two states split, Malaysia, via its national railway company KTM (Keretapi Tanah Melayu), still owned a large tract of land running through the centre of Singapore. This was an inconvenience to development, and a serious threat in the event of raised tensions between the two states. Prime Minister Lee Hsien Loong's successful resolution of the KTM railway dispute with the then Prime Minister Najib Razak is regarded as a policy hybrid. After the Points of Agreement signed under Malaysia's Prime Minister Mahathir and Lee Kuan Yew, the issue stalled under Prime Ministers Mahathir and Badawi. In the end, rather than assigning sovereignty over the land in question to one party or another, it was decided to co-develop the land under the state-owned enterprises Temasek Holdings and Khazanah Nasional. At the time this was widely seen as an innovative solution, though it has since been suggested as a way to resolve various other territorial disputes. Another example of pragmatism-as-adaptability in Singapore–Malaysia relations can be seen in the matter of water trading. Possessing inadequate fresh water of its own at the time of independence, Singapore signed three water agreements with Malaysia in 1961, 1962 and 1990, under which the Malaysian authorities would sell water to water-scarce Singapore at mutually agreed prices. The 1961 water agreement was due to expire in 2011 and, during the negotiations, the Malaysian side announced its intention to raise the raw water price.[2] Pressured to achieve water independence from Malaysia, Singapore chose to put its energy in technological innovation rather than focusing purely on negotiation strategies. As well as enhancing water catchment areas, and developing water desalination programmes, Singapore researchers invented a reverse osmosis process to 'reclaim' water from latrines.[3] This technological solution to the problem also allowed Singapore to negotiate with Malaysia from a much stronger position.

The old enemy: Learning from Japan

Despite the brutal nature of Japan's wartime occupation of Singapore, the post-independence leadership made a conscious decision to avoid reliance upon anti-Japanese sentiment as a prop to their own legitimacy – in contrast with many of their counterparts in China and Korea, for example.[4] When Japan grew into an economic giant, the Singapore leadership set aside any nationalist or personal resentment (despite many of them having experienced the occupation) and analysed the strengths of the Japanese Ministry of Trade and Industry (MITI), the role of state-led capitalism in rejuvenating the Japanese economy, and the cultural strengths of the Japanese economic programme.

Regardless of Japan's wartime record, the focus was entirely upon the lessons that could be learned from Japan's present growth. South Korea, Taiwan, Hong Kong and Singapore followed and adapted the Japanese model of state-led capitalism, in a Japanese 'flying geese formation', though with a greater or lesser willingness to admit the source of their inspiration. This story has been widely and amply accounted in business management and area studies.[5] Singapore took a 'functional' approach towards learning (i.e., learn the best of Japan) without getting emotionally fixated at Japan's past (label/form as a past conqueror, hence enemy).

Strategic pragmatism without being 3rd China: relations with China

While Lee Kuan Yew officially visited China in 1976 and Chinese President Deng Xiaoping visited Singapore in 1978, Singapore was nevertheless the last of all the ASEAN countries to officially diplomatically recognise China (1990). This reticence, despite Lee Kuan Yew's early recognition of China's future potential, was driven by a suite of practical considerations. Firstly, Singapore, with a Chinese majority population, is geographically sandwiched between Indonesia and Malaysia (both with Muslim majority populations). In view of local and regional Muslim sentiments, Singapore could not afford to be seen as a Chinese fifth column in Southeast Asia. Lily Rahim (2009) summarises the tensions thus: 'When placed within the historical context of anti-Chinese sentiment and persecution in Southeast Asia, this insecurity is not altogether surprising. In post-colonial Southeast Asia, socio-economic and political tensions have often morphed into anti-Chinese fervour, as manifested in the anti-Chinese riots in Jakarta in 1994 and 1998.'[6] Secondly, at the time China was actively promoting communism in the region with an active socialist radio channel and support provided to local communist parties such as the Malayan Communist Party (MCP). The Singaporean government was, at the time, focused on stabilising and reinforcing the 'non-ideological' status of its own domestic politics, with a particular focus on eliminating potential sources of communist ideology within the domestic sphere. The leadership reasoned that any appearance of sympathy with the People's Republic of China would be likely not merely to stir up racial tensions, but also to reignite the ideological fervour that it has taken such pains to repress. Thus, it took the apparently paradoxical strategy of adopting a hard-line position in the name of pragmatism.

Despite Singapore's late recognition of the People's Republic of China (PRC), once it became apparent that a closer relationship would be more advantageous than damaging, the rapprochement was remarkable for its speed. The Singapore–China Suzhou Industrial Park (SIP) is a case in point. In 1994, Singapore (Lee) and China (Deng) agreed to collaborate to develop the Suzhou Industrial Park; the aim was for Singapore to share its industrialisation experience with China.[7] Singapore took advantage of the international rejection of China following the Tiananmen incident to become a friend in need to the PRC government. Noting China's situation, Singapore refrained from joining the generalised chorus of moral disapproval, and rather decided to invest when the international market was bearish and thus the price of stock in 'China PLC' was low. Singapore focused on the facts – the early indicators of China's immense economic potential – and refrained from indulging in futile 'virtue signalling' on the topic of China's human rights record. The joint Suzhou Industrial Park's was set up in 1994 as a vehicle for Singapore to share expertise with China, with the backing of both Lee Kuan Yew and Deng Xiaoping. While Singapore originally held a 65% stake in the park, the decision was made to reduce this to 35% after it became apparent that local officials were planning to set up a competing park nearby and capture much of the SIP's business. Rather than risk the failure of a highly symbolic joint project, the Singapore government accepted a substantial cut in its profits in order to ensure its long-term viability. The costs inherent in dealing with the local officials and regulatory environment were judged worth absorbing in the name of reinforcing relations with the government in Beijing. Rather than making an official protest against the bad-faith actions of the local trade officials, the Singapore side chose to accept a short-term loss in exchange for potential long-term gains.[8] This overture was followed by subsequent Singapore–China projects such as the Tianjin Eco-City Project (TECP) and the Guangzhou Knowledge City project (though it is worth noting that these are relatively new projects, and their long-term future remains uncertain). In recent years, Singapore has adapted its Chinese cooperation projects to fit in with China's increasingly outward-looking economic strategy. In particular, Singaporean attention has focused on relations with Chongqing, as a means to gain the benefits of the One-Belt-One-Road initiative without incurring any of the obligations that fall upon formal participants. Chongqing is one of the key nodes in the OBOR strategy. Since the mid-2010s Singapore has increasingly focused on building closer relations with the city, and particularly in terms of financial flows and logistics – two key pillars of OBOR (One Belt One Road).[9] The China–Singapore

Connectivity Initiative (CCI), and the Southern Transport Corridor (STC) both have a clear focus on hooking Singapore into OBOR (note: OBOR term later changed to Belt Road Initiative, BRI) infrastructure while aiming to avoid any implication of vassal status.[10] Indeed, throughout this period, Singapore continued to hedge successfully, maintaining its strong relationship with the US and upholding the *modus vivendi* established with Malaysia and Indonesia, while simultaneously pursuing ever greater connections with the resurgent PRC.[11]

Between two elephants: China–US relations

"When elephants fight, the grass suffers, but when they make love, the grass suffers also."

– Lee Kuan Yew

After 1990, when Lee Kuan Yew stepped back from power and was replaced as Prime Minister by Goh Chok Tong, Singapore refrained from aligning itself with either China or the US, but rather to maintain its relations with both China and the US, albeit in different arenas. In the case of China, it was the realistic assessment of China's economic potential that instilled a desire to strengthen ties at the government-to-government and personnel levels, display Singapore's relevance to China, and establish a foothold in the Chinese economy. On the US side, Singapore sought to demonstrate its continued relevance on security issues. Thus, when the Philippines declined to renew the US rights to use the Subic Naval Base, Singapore offered the US a foothold at Changi Naval Base. This was linked to greater security and technological exchanges between the US and Singapore.[12] Once again, we see a perceived need in Singapore policy to not merely adopt Big-P pragmatism in its policy-making processes, but also to perform it. In other words, under such conditions, pragmatism must not merely be done, but be seen to be done. In a situation in which political and civil service advancement can be dependent upon the perceptions of one's peers and superiors regarding one's pragmatism or lack thereof, situations can arise in which politicians and civil servants receive greater rewards for enacting decisions that fit the received ideas of what pragmatism is, even if they are not actually pragmatic with regard to the circumstances of the times.

During Lee Hsien Loong's era, the room for manoeuvre between the US and China shrunk, as China rose and the two nations increasingly began to clash over trade policy and military issues in the South and East China Seas, and yet Singapore continued to maintain the pragmatic principle of duality.[13] Despite extending Changi Naval Base to the US, which is large enough to accommodate US nuclear aircraft carriers, recently, Singapore pragmatically extended the same privilege to the PLA Navy, with the Prime Minister's Office choosing to make the information public.[14] The intent was clearly to demonstrate that Singapore had not chosen a side, and wished instead to be accommodating to both powers.

As China has grown increasingly assertive, the strategic landscape has become increasingly difficult to navigate. Singapore has started increasing its security cooperation with China. While tangible security cooperation has tended to be limited to anti-terrorism issues and focused predominantly on low-technology operations so as not to compromise technological transfer agreements with the US, the middle ground has grown increasingly narrow.[15] As China has increasingly begun to come into conflict with other powers regarding the issue of control over the South China Sea, Singapore has come under increasing pressure to take a side.[16] Rather than do this, Singapore has attempted to walk an ever narrower line of neutrality, a process rendered all the more complex by the fact that it is an ethnically Chinese majority state. While this can be helpful in dealing with China – providing a large stock of diplomats fluent in the language and knowledgeable about cultural codes – it can also lead to Singapore coming under suspicion as a potential Chinese fifth column in Southeast Asia.[17] In the future, it is likely that both China and the US will want to demand exclusive loyalty from Singapore, with Singapore finding it increasingly difficult to keep both suitors interested while committing to neither.[18]

Without humane feelings: Singapore and Cambodia

The trend of hedging between the US and China can be seen in the manoeuvring around the use of Changi Naval Base, but even more clearly in the Singaporean handling of the Cambodian conflict.

This case is of particular interest because it saw Singapore adopting a conventionally liberal international position for thoroughly pragmatic reasons – an excellent illustration of the argument that the proper unit of analysis in studies of pragmatism is the decision rather than the individual or the institution, as described in the introduction earlier. While the defence of international law and a preference for democratic institutions are traditionally seen within international relations theory as liberal causes, the Singapore government adopted these positions based on its assessment of its own interests, rather than for ideological reasons, and was entirely up-front about doing so. As S.R. Nathan puts it:

> *'The Kampuchean issue was central to Singapore's policy. The principle involved was that no foreign military intervention should be allowed to*

overthrow a legally constituted regime. If this principle was violated, it would create a dangerous precedent. Foreign forces could go into Thailand and depose the current Thai government and put up a regime under the Communist Party of Thailand. Singapore had to work on the worst possible outcome. With this in mind, Singapore could not compromise.[19]

In other words, as in its domestic pursuit of economic prosperity, the protection of international law was seen as being of sufficient importance that short-run compromises in other areas would be a price worth paying to achieve it – the 'most takes all' reasoning that was a central feature of pragmatism as defined by Lee Kuan Yew and his closest lieutenants.[20] Indeed, the then Foreign Minister Dhanabalan described the Cambodian conflict as 'the key issue for the Ministry', while Goh Keng Swee referred to it as 'a life-and-death struggle, the outcome of which will have a profound effect on the Republic'.[21]

After the fall of Saigon in 1975, the Singapore leadership's principal fear was that the Vietnamese Communist leadership would be emboldened by their success and launch upon an expansionist policy within the region, threatening or invading Laos and Cambodia, and putting pressure on Thailand and Malaysia. The possibility of Communist-inspired insurgencies within the countries involved working to bring about such an outcome had immediate implications for a leadership group already engaged in a campaign of fierce repression against its own internal communist opposition.

Thus, while the protection of international law is classically seen as an idealistic goal, Singapore's subtle role in the efforts within ASEAN and at the United Nations to condemn Vietnam's invasion of Cambodia and the removal of the Khmer Rouge regime was a product of pragmatism rather than lofty ideals. The key principle that Singapore wished to uphold at the time was that of state sovereignty; an understandable principle for a small state to espouse, given their historical vulnerability under non-Westphalian regimes.

Singapore's position was thus a product of its distinctive geographic situation. While counterfactual reasoning is a dubious exercise, it seems reasonable to assume that the same leadership team in charge of a far bigger state would have cared little for a small state sovereignty and the tenets of international law. Minister Dhanabalan explained the position in pragmatic terms,[22] noting that, however unsavoury the Cambodian leadership may have been, Singapore's interest in defending international law trumped any desire to avoid associating with individuals that they privately disliked.[23] Singapore's leadership, accordingly, did their best to defend Cambodian sovereignty without necessarily aligning themselves with the Cambodian leadership.

In practice, the Singaporean position expressed itself through two strategic efforts:

(1) Shaping international and regional opinion: Various explanations of this strategy, penned by S R Nathan, Tommy Koh, Barry Desker and Ang Cheng Guan, have covered Singapore's role in shaping regional and international opinion via closed-door diplomacy.[24] This strategy was broadly successful. ASEAN was convinced and demanded Vietnam's immediate withdrawal, a position that was supported by China and the US (albeit for various reasons). The United Nations officially condemned Vietnam's actions, and recognised Democratic Kampuchea as a member-state of the UN General Assembly.

(2) Supporting elections in Cambodia: Singapore pragmatically took care to avoid stating any preference for a specific leader or enforcing a particular style of election or governance. This realism-inspired strategy was rewarded with a broadly satisfactory outcome; the Paris Peace talks started in 1989, an agreement was signed in 1991, with the United Nations Transitional Authority of Cambodia (UNTAC) formed in 1992 to supervise elections, and the elections were completed in 1993. A constitutional monarchy was restored with Prince Sihanouk as the head of state, his son Prince Ranariddh as the first Prime Minister and Hun Sen as the second Prime Minister.

A policy of quiet support for any and all Cambodian governments while simultaneously opposing outside intervention was thus pursued from the 1960s onwards, from the first Sihanouk government, through the Lon Nol years, and even during the humanitarian abuses of the Khmer Rouge regime. This policy was prosecuted as a principle, being key to the national interest, despite the profound personal misgivings of the Singapore leadership concerning their interlocutors at any given time. Lee Kuan Yew was always careful to state support for the Khmer people's right to self-determination, rather than for any particular government, and was frequently publicly disparaging of groups or individuals, describing the Khmer Rouge leadership in general as 'insane' and Hun Sen in particular as 'utterly merciless and lacking in humane feelings'.[25]

The overall result was that Singapore's diplomatic efforts both within ASEAN and internationally helped to intensify lukewarm foreign opposition to Vietnam's expansionism. This combined with the lack of military success and the collapse of the Soviet Union ensured that by 1991 Bilahari Kausikan could conclude that there was 'no longer a need for Singapore to take an activist posture on the Cambodian issue. Our approach now is to extricate ourselves. For the last year, we have in fact begun a process of diplomatic disengagement from the Cambodian issue. In Indochina, our priority is now to develop bilateral relations with Vietnam.'[26]

Just as Singapore had been willing to work for the benefit of a regime that its leaders disliked intensely, it was also more than happy to forge mutually beneficial connections with an old adversary – Vietnam – once its ability to threaten national security had been eliminated.

Ok, but now what?

Concrete examples of policy-making are of limited utility without an over-reaching theory or framework to unite and underpin them. In the next chapter, we will do our best to extrapolate the most salient features of the cases described in the previous two sections, with the aim of distilling Singaporean pragmatism down to its purest essence.

Notes

1 Lee Khoon Choy (1993). *Diplomacy of a Tiny State*. Singapore: World Scientific: p. 271.
2 Accessed from: http://eresources.nlb.gov.sg/infopedia/articles/SIP_1533_2009-06-23.html. Accessed on 31 March 2019.
3 Reverse osmosis is pioneered by Hyflux, a Singapore-based once-Temasek-linked company.
4 Cho Il Hyun and Park Seo-Hyun (2011). "Anti-Chinese and Anti-Japanese sentiments in East Asia: The Politics of Opinion, Distrust, and Prejudice." *The Chinese Journal of International Politics*, Vol. 4, No. 3, pp. 265–290.
5 John Wong (2009). "East Asian Experiences of Economic Development." *East Asian Policy*, Vol. 1, No. 4, October–December, pp. 48–54.
6 Lily Zubaidah Rahim (2009). *Singapore in the Malay World: Building and Breaching Regional Bridges*. Oxon: Routledge: p. 58.
7 Accessed from: www.straitstimes.com/asia/east-asia/suzhou-industrial-park-10-things-to-know-about-the-china-singapore-project. Accessed on 9 November 2017.
8 Lam Chuan Leong (2015). *Up Close with Lee Kuan Yew: Insights from Colleagues and Friends*. Singapore: Marshall Cavendish: pp. 155–158.
9 Accessed from: www.channelnewsasia.com/news/singapore/chongqing-connectivity-initiative-can-be-testbed-for-new-policie-7823664. Accessed on 9 November 2017.
10 Chan Chun Sing, "Speech at the Future China Global Forum and Singapore Regional Business Forum 2018," MTI, 28 August 2018. Accessed from: www.mti.gov.sg/Newsroom/Speeches/2018/08/Speech-by-Minister-Chan-Chun-Sing-at-the-CCI-STC-Seminar-2018. Accessed on 4 May 2019.
11 Shashi Jayakumar and Rahul Sagar (2015). *The Big Ideas of Lee Kuan Yew*. Singapore: Straits Times Press: p. 160.
12 Goh Chok Tong, LKYSPP 13rd Anniversary Lecture, 8 September 2017.
13 Interview with Su Ge, 9 March 2017.

14 Elgin Toh (2017). "Singapore Must Work Hard at Staying Relevant: Chan Chun Sing." *Straits Times*, 31 October 2017.

15 Interview with Ma Zhenggang, 2 March 2017.

16 John J. Mearsheimer (2010). "The Gathering Storm: China's Challenge to US Power in Asia." *The Chinese Journal of International Politics*, Vol. 3, No. 4, pp. 381–396.

17 Irene Ng (2010). *The Singapore Lion: A Biography of S. Rajaratnam*. Singapore: Institute of Southeast Asian Studies.

18 Robyn Klingler-Vidra (2012). *The Pragmatic 'Little Red Dot': Singapore's US Hedge Against China*. London: LSE IDEAS.

19 Ang Cheng Guan (2013). *Singapore, ASEAN and the Cambodian Conflict 1978–1991*. Singapore: NUS Press.

20 Liew Mun Leong, Speech at the Lee Kuan Yew School of Public Policy, 27 March 2019.

21 Ang Cheng Guan (2013). *Singapore, ASEAN and the Cambodian Conflict 1978–1991*. Singapore: NUS Press: p. 5.

22 Interview with Suppiah Dhanabalan, 17 January 2019.

23 Lee Kuan Yew, hardly a bleeding-heart liberal himself, was known to have described Cambodian leader Hun Sen and his colleagues as "utterly merciless and ruthless, without humane feelings".

24 See, for example: Barry Desker, "Against All Odds: Singapore's Successful Lobbying on the Cambodia Issue at the United Nations." *Occasional Paper*, ISEAS Press, Singapore, 2016.

25 Ang Cheng Guan (2013). *Singapore, ASEAN and the Cambodian Conflict 1978–1991*. Singapore: NUS Press: p. 10.

26 Ang Cheng Guan (2013). *Singapore, ASEAN and the Cambodian Conflict 1978–1991*. Singapore: NUS Press: p. 155.

12 The geography of pragmatism

Many academics and practitioners have described Singapore as pragmatic, but many omitted to explain what pragmatism in Singapore means in any detail, even though the authors themselves had multiple interpretations of the term. In his book *Singapore: Identity, Brand, Power*, Kenneth Paul Tan summarised the most frequently implied conceptualisations of the term: 'acting in a non-dogmatic but instrumental way', having 'little patience for philosophy, theory, or finely nuanced and elaborate arguments', being 'willing to learn . . . from best practices available anywhere in the world', taking 'a realist perspective on human nature', having 'little patience for intangible, even qualitative, values in its materialist world', and being 'managerial in . . . orientation to leadership'.[1] As Tan noted, pragmatism tends to have specific connotations when used in a foreign policy context, effectively functioning as a synonym for 'realist' most of the time.

While many analyses of Singaporean policy-making (particularly those produced by leaders or former leaders) have taken official declarations of adherence to purely pragmatic strategies at face value, others have taken the position that, perversely, the Singapore government's obsessive focus on pragmatic policy-making has, over time, worked to create a state 'ideology of pragmatism'. As Tan argued: 'By doggedly describing itself as pragmatic, the Singapore state is actually disguising its ideological work and political nature through an assertion of the absence of ideology and politics.'[2] In other words, pragmatism has effectively taken on the same function as ideology occupies in ideological states: not merely to guide political strategy, but also to justify political decisions, irrespective of their actual content. The Singapore narrative is: Singapore is only a city-state, with no hinterland, we must work to be 'at the table, not on the menu',[3] we must be pragmatic to survive.[4] In this respect, pragmatism has been institutionalised in the mindset of the bureaucracy and the leadership, and the selection of candidates for future leadership in bureaucracy and politics using a suite of

DOI: 10.4324/9781003202721-15

measures that includes perceived pragmatism further deepens the institutionalisation of the ideology of pragmatism at high levels.

While the Singapore government's fixation on pragmatic policy-making was originally a logical response to the difficult circumstances that prevailed immediately following independence, it later became an article of faith and a way to prevent criticism, with developmental authoritarian attitudes towards politics prevailing long after development had been achieved.

The focus on pragmatism in analysing Singapore's political decision-making can be traced back to the beliefs of the founding fathers, Lee Kuan Yew and Goh Keng Swee. As Lee Kuan Yew said in a 1994 Parliament speech, 'If a thing works, let's work it, and that eventually evolved into the kind of economy that we have today [sic]. Our test was: Does it work?'[5] Similarly, in 1977, Goh Keng Swee emphasised the importance of practical benefits over signalling: 'It might have been politically tempting to rid ourselves of institutions and practices that bore, or seemed to bear, the taint of colonial associations. Had we done so we would have thrown away a priceless advantage for the sake of empty rhetoric.'[6] Over time the pragmatic tendencies of the founding fathers have been in-grained within the culture of both the PAP and the civil service, as described by Neo Boon Siong and Geraldine Chen: 'The founding generation of leaders – Lee Kuan Yew, Goh Keng Swee, and, to a certain extent, Hon Sui Sen – in their own ways, shaped the ethos and values of the Singapore public service, and the way it defined and approached its key functions.'[7]

Singapore's foreign policy is frequently described as 'realist'. Michael Leifer's 'Coping with Vulnerability' is generally seen as the defining work on Singapore's realist foreign policy.[8] Leifer was a realist in outlook. His thesis was essentially that Singapore is small and had to cope with vulnerability, and hence has been obliged to take a realist position. While his work is useful, his position cannot adequately explain the occasional liberal tendencies of Singapore's foreign policy and its dedication to 'economic interdependence and regional institution-building'.[9]

It is, of course, entirely possible that such academic interpretations are over-analysing a fundamentally simple concept in ways that would have seemed alien to its progenitors. Tommy Koh, for example, in a eulogy for Lee Kuan Yew in March 2015 described the first principle of Singapore's foreign policy as pragmatism:

> *'First, our foreign policy is based on pragmatism and not on any doctrine or ideology. The scholars who have written that Singapore's foreign policy is based on realism are mistaken. If it were based on realism, we would not have attached so much importance to international law or to the United Nations. Our constant lodestar is to promote the security and prosperity of Singapore.'*[10]

Similarly, Prime Minister Lee Hsien Loong summarised the key fundamentals behind Singapore's foreign relations, concluding that 'Singapore can continue to be the master of its own destiny on the global stage by adopting a "balance between realism and idealism" to defend and advance its interests abroad.'[11]

This chapter aims to use the case studies analysed previously to steer a middle course, and create a definition of Singapore pragmatism that reflects both the nuance and outsider perspectives to be found in academic analyses, and the intentions of its founding fathers.

The ideology of the poisonous shrimp

As described earlier, much of the Singapore leadership's attachment to pragmatic politics was based on perceived vulnerability – a product of the country's small size and lack of resources. In other words, Singapore's ideology of pragmatism has been institutionalised in the name of national survival, predicated upon a perceived sense of vulnerability when faced with much larger neighbours and a lack of domestic resources. The over-arching goal was always simply that of being left alone: as Lee Kuan Yew put it, Singapore was forced to become a "poison shrimp" to avoid being eaten by bigger fish. It is interesting to compare the role of external pressures in Singapore's pragmatism with the waxing and waning of pragmatism in Chinese politics. As we saw earlier, Chinese leaders have tended to become more pragmatic when under less pressure, and more ideological when facing urgent threats. Singapore, by contrast, experienced the opposite phenomenon, with the leadership focusing on pragmatism as a result of external pressures. The reliance upon pragmatism as a panacea for all pressing problems has led to its gradual assumption of many of the attributes of an ideology. Today, though many of the external pressures that led to its adoption have evolved, the ideal of pragmatism remains an article of faith among Singapore's politicians and bureaucrats.

Notes from a small island

Geography has generally been the most important factor influencing Singapore's perception of its own lack of power and hence of its sense of vulnerability. Its small size originally made it a 'price-taker nation' – with a relative lack of negotiating power. While this factor has been remedied to a large degree through its rapid growth, and the possession of a currency, an army and a sovereign wealth fund that punch well above their weight, the siege mentality has remained constant, as described earlier.[12] At independence, as lack of natural resources has rendered its continued survival dependent upon the goodwill of other states, in the sense that lacked the option of self-sufficiency that is available (if not necessarily appealing) to larger states possessing an agricultural hinterland, hydrocarbons and metal resources. Together, this translated into a particular conception of its place in the world: Singapore's existence was not a given, and the nation-state had to constantly strive to ensure its relevance to the rest of the world, and to specific great powers such as the US and China, whilst maintaining its sovereign status. As such, it had an understandable preference for multipolarity. As Singapore's first Foreign Minister, S. Rajaratnam, puts it: "Like the sun, the great powers will, by their very existence, radiate gravitational power. But if there are many suns then the smaller planets can, by judicious balancing of pulls and counter-pulls, enjoy a greater freedom of movement."[13]

Singapore's status as a land-scarce and largely encircled state also influenced its relatively strong line on national sovereignty (see Singapore's pro-active diplomacy behind ASEAN and the UN's condemnation of Vietnam's invasion of Cambodia, as described earlier). The fact that Singapore is a Chinese majority state sandwiched between larger states with Muslim majorities (Indonesia and Malaysia) has tended to compound the siege mentality and Singapore's cautious navigation of the Malay world (Rahim, 2010),[14] as well as influencing Singapore's decision to be the last Southeast Asian state to officially recognise China (as referenced earlier).

While history and socio-cultural factors have played a role in fostering pragmatism, they in turn are strongly influenced by geography, meaning that the latter can be said to be the root cause. The senior PAP leadership in the early years openly asserted the predominance of geography in determining their strategic orientations, and while Singapore's political system is pluralistic (with various weak actors), the dominant leader (Prime Minister) is the strongest agent, and plays a disproportionate role in setting the agenda for other actors. Civil society does not comment on foreign policy, and social media is also relatively quiet on foreign policy issues. The traditional media focuses almost entirely on factual reporting, with commentators who express inconvenient opinions on foreign policy issues risking their careers by doing so.[15] Even the opposition generally agrees with the incumbent government on foreign policy direction. For example, in 2017, the then-Secretary-General of the Workers' Party Low Thia Kiang gave a speech about rising China's implications to Singapore's place in the world. Low identified Singapore's foreign policy position as well as strategic partners, and then questioned if 'our foreign policy principles need to be updated in view of the changing world order.' The speech drew praise from both the Foreign Minister and Prime Minister Lee Hsien Loong on their Facebook accounts. PM Lee wrote: 'Some opposition MPs made good speeches too. Mr Low Thia Kiang set out succinctly how the strategic landscape is changing, and how this challenges our foreign policy. He asked: how can we protect and advance the national interest of our multi-racial country?' Foreign minister Vivian Balakrishnan also noted that Low posed a 'thoughtful question' reflecting the level of 'bipartisan support for our foreign policy efforts.'[16]

In Singapore, in other words, 'politics stops at the water's edge' with politicians, regardless of party affiliation, being united on foreign policy aims and broad strategies. This, in itself, works to reinforce the PAP's dominance over national narratives and conceptual frameworks, with the ideal of a strong leader required to preserve a vulnerable state eventually becoming self-perpetuating.

Singapore's small size and lack of natural resources have always been cited in the national narrative to justify why Singapore must be thankful that it is still in existence, that Singaporeans must work hard and not take survival and prosperity for granted, and that the government must be strong, relatively unchallenged, constantly think and plan ahead, and execute with caution. This mantra is deeply pragmatic, and yet it is also an ideology, and the narrative is a dogma that is taught in national education, as well as being perpetuated via homophily in the selection of talent in the bureaucracy and the political system and the training offered to those selected.

People like us

Elite homophily is likely to have been the dominant factor behind the institutionalisation of the ideology of pragmatism. It is not surprising that a government wedded to an 'ideology of pragmatism' will be likely to attract, select and promote new members who embody the same values. The assessment criteria used in assessing civil servants have traditionally been summarised under the HAIR acronym (Helicopter, Analysis, Imagination, Reality), all of which were strongly linked to the government's self-perceptions: 'helicopter' referred to the ability to see the Big-Picture – to take a bird's eye view of any given issue. Analysis means the application of economic cost–benefit analysis approaches to aid decision-making. Imagination and reality (or realism) referred to the ability to come up with solutions that are both creative and practical. The use of these highly pragmatic values to select candidates for high office has contributed to the institutionalisation of the Singaporean ideology of pragmatism. With knowledge of such selection criteria, even those with ideological preferences of their own are liable to be influenced by a desire for personal advancement or conformity to align themselves with the government. Politicians and civil servants who appear to embody these pragmatic values will likely be absorbed into the national elite and promoted quickly within the system.

In a similar vein, once accepted into the party or bureaucratic system, recruits tend to find themselves encouraged to pursue training in fields that are perceived to be of solid practical use to the party and/or the nation. During the developmental phase of Singapore's existence, the early cohorts of scholars within the Public Service Commission were only permitted to study engineering.[17] This included functionaries in apparently unrelated fields, such as foreign affairs – thus, career diplomats such as Kishore Mahbubani ended up with at least some experience of studying more 'practical' fields. In later years, while more freedom was given to civil servants and other leaders wishing to pursue education, the focus tended to be on economics, reflecting both the economic training of the relevant generation of leaders and the perceived need for economic skills in government as state management of the national economy grew more data-driven and the financial sector grew to make up a much bigger part of the national GDP.[18]

Pragmatism: A self-reinforcing belief?

Singapore's pragmatic foreign policy was the fruit of its geographical constraints, insofar as the adaptive, unsentimental approach to politics taken by Lee Kuan Yew and his early lieutenants can be said to be a strategically reasonable response to trying circumstances. Over time, however, pragmatism has been transformed from a spontaneous response to a specific set of geographical constraints into a fully-fledged state ideology, being used to justify and perpetuate the PAP's strong authoritarian leadership. The ideology of pragmatism has become ever more entrenched, via the selection of talent that reflects the personal and political qualities that earlier generations of leaders valued in themselves.

Thus, it can be seen that pragmatism has been a choice – if a heavily coerced choice – for Singapore to a much greater degree than for its Chinese counterparts. While Chinese leaders have tended to swing between ideology and pragmatism as a reflection of the survival pressures they faced, successive Singapore governments have chosen (more or less consciously) to hold onto it, despite the gradual disappearance of the pressures that compelled its adoption in the first place.

While China's technocratic system of institutions has, since the death of Mao Zedong, done much to compel pragmatic reasoning on the part of his successors, Singapore's hybrid democracy does not occupy the same function. While it may seem unlikely at the time of going to press, it would not be impossible under Singapore's current institutional arrangements for an ideological populist leader to emerge and win power. From the point of view of the supporters of pragmatism within the administration and elsewhere, this would be seen as a disaster. To understand how to counter such a policy (without resorting to Chinese-style authoritarianism), it is necessary to look westward, to the United States.

Notes

1 Kenneth Paul Tan (2018). *Singapore: Identity, Brand, Power*. Cambridge: Cambridge University Press: pp. 17–19.
2 Kenneth Paul Tan (2018). *Singapore: Identity, Brand, Power*. Cambridge: Cambridge University Press: pp. 17–19.
3 S. Jayakumar (2015). *Be at the Table or Be on the Menu: A Singapore Memoir*. Singapore: Straits Times Press.
4 Interview with Lim Siong Guan, 3 April 2017.
5 Lee Kuan Yew, Speech in Parliament on the White Paper on Ministerial Salaries on 1 November 1994, as cited in Han Fook Kwang, W. Fernandez and S. Tan (Eds.) (1998). *Lee Kuan Yew: The Man and His Ideas*. Singapore: Times Editions: p. 109.
6 Goh Keng Swee (1977 and 1995) as cited in Ian Patrick Austin (2004). *Goh Keng Swee and Southeast Asian Governance*. Singapore: Marshall Cavendish Academic, as quoted in Neo Boon Siong and Geraldine Chen (2007). *Dynamic Governance: Embedding Culture, Capabilities and Change in Singapore*. Singapore: World Scientific: pp. 166–167.
7 Neo and Chen, 2007. Jon S. T. Quah (2010). *Public Administration Singapore Style*. Singapore: Talisman: pp. 147–148.
8 Bilveer Singh (1999). *The Vulnerability of Small States Revisited: A Study of Singapore's Post-Cold War Foreign Policy*. Yogyakarta: Gadjah Mada University Press. Chan Heng Chee (1988). *Singapore: Domestic Structure and Foreign Policy: Final Draft*. Kawin Wilairat (1975). *Singapore's Foreign Policy*. Singapore: ISEAS Press. Alan Chong (2006). "Singapore's Foreign Policy Beliefs as 'Abridged Realism': Pragmatic and Liberal Prefixes in the Foreign Policy Thought of Rajaratnam, Lee, Koh and Mahbubani." *International Relations of the Asia Pacific*, Vol. 6, No. 2.
9 Acharya Amitav (2008). *Singapore's Foreign Policy: The Search for Regional Order*. Singapore: World Scientific.
10 Tommy Koh (2015). "Remembering Lee Kuan Yew: Our Chief Diplomat to the World." *Straits Times*, 25 March 2015. Accessed from: www.straitstimes.com/singapore/remembering-lee-kuan-yew-our-chief-diplomat-to-the-world. Accessed on 31 March 2019.
11 Chong Zi Liang (2015). "Singapore Diplomacy 50 Years on." *Straits Times*, 6 December 2015. Accessed from: www.straitstimes.com/politics/singapore-diplomacy-50-years-on. Accessed on 31 March 2019.
12 Kishore Mahbubani (2017). "Treat China and Trump with Respect in 2017." *Straits Times*, 11 February 2017.
13 S. Rajaratnam (1973). *Speech to the Asia Society*. New York.
14 Lily Zubaidah Rahim (2010). *Singapore in the Malay World: Building and Breaching Regional Bridges*. Oxon: Routledge: p. 58.

15 Yip Wai Yee (2017). "Mediacorp Apologises for Remarks on Najib in TV Show." *Straits Times*, 6 April 2017.

16 Tanya Ong (2018). "Number of Times PAP Praise Opposition Few and Far Between but It's Has Happened Before." *Mothership*, 16 May 2018. Accessed from: https://mothership.sg/2018/05/pap-praising-opposition-history. Accessed on 31 March 2019.

17 Interview with Lim Siong Guan, 3 April 2017.

18 Interview with Lim Siong Guan, 3 April 2017.

Part IV
The United States

13 The system (systemic pendulums) of pragmatism

"The test of first-rate intelligence is the ability to hold two opposed in mind at the same time and still retain the ability to function."

– F. Scott Fitzgerald

This chapter, like those above, focuses on the interplay of Small and Big-P pragmatism in the internal and external policy-making of the state under consideration. In it, we intend to define and describe a different form of interaction between the two concepts than those covered in the previous chapters. While the China case looked at individuals' transitions from Small to Big-P pragmatism across the course of their careers, and the Singapore case showed that Big-P pragmatism can become Small-P over time if not careful, the present case intends to demonstrate that the aggregate of many Small-P pragmatic decisions can be a Big-P pragmatic decision, if the system in which they take place forces such an outcome.

Many authors have tried to define the US as a realist or liberal foreign policy power. Indeed, the fact that the argument has gone on for so long suggests in itself that there is something to be said in favour of both interpretations, but that neither provides a complete explanation.

In fact, US foreign policy is best summed up as a product of the co-existence of realism and idealism. The exact configuration of this co-existence depends on the circumstances. There is a strong pendulum effect in US foreign policy; most administrations will start off with a more ideological stance, reflecting their position during the election campaign that brought them to power, before gradually becoming more pragmatic as the weight of circumstances begins to tell.

DOI: 10.4324/9781003202721-17

Pragmatism by the book: A little navel-gazing

There exists an extensive literature on US diplomatic history and foreign relations, covering foreign and defence policy, foreign policy thinking, grand strategy (or the absence thereof), and even several works specifically dealing with pragmatism and ideology in US foreign policy. This ranges from factual accounts with some interpretation to those focusing on the vision, principles, values, strategies and tactics used. Other literature focuses more on the conceptual assumptions of different policy 'factions', whether arguing in favour of one school or another or simply comparing the various perspectives. Grand strategy elevates foreign policy and thinking upwards to assess if there is an overarching strategy that guides policy actions. This chapter will focus on the dominant foreign policy frameworks, and particularly on existing frameworks surrounding pragmatism and their gaps.

US foreign policy thinking has produced a variety of conceptual frameworks, of which Walter Russell Mead's four paradigms are probably the best-known.[1] Mead divided foreign policy thinking into Hamiltonian, Wilsonian, Jeffersonian, and Jacksonian strands, and covers their evolution through US history. These were later summarised by Perry Anderson as the "Hamiltonian pursuit of commercial advantage for American enterprise abroad; Wilsonian duty to extend the values of liberty across the world; Jeffersonian concern to preserve the virtues of the Republic from foreign temptations; and Jacksonian valour in any challenge to the honour or security of the country."[2] While Mead was cautious to note that actual foreign policy behaviour could cut across the four paradigms according to context, Anderson saw the positions more as belonging to different sections of society: "If the first two were elite creeds, and the third an inclination among intellectuals, the fourth was the folk ethos of the majority of the American people."[3]

By contrast, Walter A. McDougall emphasised (and condemned) the role of Christianity in shaping US foreign policy, seeing strategy as strongly influenced by religious ideology, creating positions based on delusions of grandeur and a sentiment of having been "chosen" by God.[4] However, McDougall does little to distinguish this tendency from other claims to exceptionalism expressed by other successful hegemonic powers in the past, or delve extensively into the pragmatic advantages to be gained through the possession of a unifying ideology. A similar role was assigned to religion by Andrew Preston and Yu Ge in their respective analyses.[5] Meanwhile, Tony Smith espoused a similar but more secular idea, attributing recent foreign policy failures to delusions of grandeur inspired by the Wilsonian belief in the inevitability of a liberal international order.[6] This vision is shared to a degree by Michael Hunt, who saw ideology as the translation of a culturally embedded sense of national greatness combined with a belief in racial hierarchy.[7]

Studies of US pragmatism are frequently framed as a counterpoint to visions of the US as a largely ideological foreign policy entity. John G. Stoessinger wrote the foundational analysis of ideological and pragmatic viewpoints in US foreign policy, breaking leaders down in an either/or fashion into "crusaders" and "pragmatists" based on their personal histories and decisions made while in power.[8] Colin Dueck picked up the same theme in his work, *Reluctant Crusaders*, but rather saw each individual as being pulled in opposite directions by ideology and contingency. In particular, Dueck emphasises the perceived need for prospective leaders to emphasise strong ideological positions in order to win votes, before walking back their stance in the face of the practicalities of day-to-day dealings with other nations.[9] Stephen Walt took a similar position, blaming the US's "immature" foreign policy on the pressures of the democratic system: "The US brings in a new team every time the White House switches parties. Americans remain remarkably ignorant of the world they believe it is their obligation and destiny to run, and the topic of foreign affairs captures public attention only when major mistakes have already been made. . . . The US allowed its foreign policy to be distorted by partisan sniping, hijacked by foreign lobbyists and narrow domestic special interests; blinded by lofty but unrealistic rhetoric."[10]

By contrast, Cecil Crabb saw the US as a predominantly pragmatic power, arguing that the US conflictual democratic model trains leaders in pragmatism (or compels them to accept it) in the domestic sphere, a habit that they carry over to their international dealings.[11] This vision was directly contradicted by Paul R. Pillar, however, who argued that while US politicians may be thoroughly pragmatic in internal affairs, a disconnect born of distance frequently leads them to adopt an unrealistically ideological position in the international sphere.[12]

It can also be instructive to study foreign perspectives on US pragmatism. Yu Huaiyan, for instance, defines and describes US pragmatism from a Chinese perspective, focusing on the search for efficiency based on real-world experience, a perspective borrowed from the business sector.[13]

Finally, the "Kissinger tradition" of weighty eulogies to US pragmatism by former exponents is noteworthy for its extent if not always for its objectivity; the fact that such a position is capable of selling books implies in itself that devotion to ideology is not the only ideal capable of attracting adherents in US foreign policy discussion. Indeed, seen from such a perspective, pragmatism can often appear to have the characteristics of an ideology. It is also worth noting that in recent years, pragmatism has often been wrapped into or displaced by "smart power" as defined by Joseph Nye, a trend that has spawned a new and extensive branch of analysis.[14] Why suddenly we go heavy on the literature review? In stark contrast to China Singapore chapters though.

The line between ideology and pragmatism is most frequently blurred at the grand strategy level, with little agreement – even now – on whether the Cold War was the product primarily of ideological incompatibility or great power rivalry. Ionut Popescu argues that the US grand strategy has often been at its best when at its least "grand" – that is to say, when influenced more by contingency than by a teleological vision, a position largely supported by Hal Brands in *What Good is Grand Strategy?*[15] Much of the time, however, the assumptions upon which a grand strategy is built are strongly influenced by cultural beliefs, which can in turn be seen as a form of ideology.[16] Indeed, the US scholarly and foreign policy fascination with grand strategy can be seen by itself as a reflection of a nation whose size and relative power have afforded it the luxury to indulge itself in philosophising about issues that other nations perceive purely in terms of day-to-day survival.[17]

Swinging both ways: the US pragmatism pendulum in practice

As mentioned earlier, US foreign policy frequently experiences a pendulum effect, swinging from pragmatic to ideological and back again. This can be – as suggested by Dueck and Walt above – the product of individual politicians emphasising hard-line position during the campaign stage and then being obliged to compromise once in office. Or, in alternative terms, being ideological during agenda-setting and pragmatic in policy-formulation/ implementation. However, it can also be seen in terms of more long-term cycles, as an ideological president comes to be seen as doctrinaire and inflexible, and is then replaced with a more pragmatic one, who eventually comes to be seen as shallow and ineffectual. Christopher Layne produced an extensive analysis of this trend from the Second World War onwards, focusing on swings from unilateralism to multilateralism and back again.[18] In a similar exercise, Christopher Hemmer described the swing as being between values and interests.[19]

The following chapter will take a series of case studies from US–China relations, to demonstrate the continued prevalence of the pendulum effect, at both the micro and macro levels, within and across presidential terms. We suggest that history shows that campaigning candidates tend to take hard-line stances with regard to China as a useful way of demonstrating their toughness to the electorate, regardless of the low likelihood of success in obtaining their putative goals. Historically, tough measures against China have tended to be ineffective in achieving their aims, simply because of China's ability to absorb all but the most extreme foreign sanctions with relative equanimity. As Winston Churchill famously observed: 'punishing China is like flogging a jellyfish'. For this reason, talk of sanctions and tariffs tends to be more about domestic display than about obtaining policy concessions. Once in office, a combination of internal and external factors generally obliges them to take a more conciliatory approach. Whether this is done via a quiet walking-back of previous positions or vaunted as a successful reconciliation depends upon the administration, but the pragmatic abandonment of idealistic campaign promises when faced with the difficulties of carrying them out is an observable long-run trend.

While the Johnson administration adopted relatively hard-line rhetoric in addressing China's role in Vietnam – despite real-world uncertainty concerning the precise extent of Chinese involvement – Nixon took a much more conciliatory approach.[20] This was largely pursued by Ford, but foreign policy opinion had begun to split by the time Carter took office, with the President leaning towards the view that any attempt to pursue a closer relationship with China would be liable to destabilise US–Soviet relations.[21] The pendulum continued on its arc as Carter was replaced by Reagan, who campaigned on an anti-China ticket but later became less rigid on the topic.[22]

However, as described earlier, the pendulum effect is often apparent within presidential terms, and not merely from president to president. As part of Ronald Reagan's anti-China policies, he backed the sale of FX fighters to Taiwan, which sparked off a crisis only alleviated by the August 1982 US–China Joint Communiqué with the US vaguely limiting arms sales to Taiwan and China agreeing to seek a 'peaceful solution'.[23] In the end, the pendulum swung so far that Reagan visited China and became the first American President to address the Great Hall of People in Apr 1984.[24] Discussions for the Communiqué started in Jan 1982, implying that Reagan took only one year to absorb the realities of US-China relations and reverse his campaign rhetoric.

A similar effect could be observed under Clinton. In 1992, he had criticised George Bush Sr. for 'coddling dictators', and opposed renewal of China's most-favoured nation status for human rights reasons.[25] As President, he pursued this policy via a May 1993 executive order explicitly linking the two. However, this was quickly reversed. By May 1994, he was describing "tough human rights policy [as] hampering the US in pursuing other interests".[26] As in the Reagan case, this reversal took around one year to realise the realities and make a virtue of necessity by adopting a more conciliatory tone with China. Thereafter, Clinton seemingly decided that the best way to encourage greater respect for human rights in China was through mutually beneficial trade: 'engage China but take a firm line', 'fair trade will liberalise China', 'spur China reforms through PNTR [permanent normal trade relations, renewed version of most-favoured nation status which Clinton signed in US–China Relations Act in Oct 2000[27]] and China in the WTO'.[28]

Bush Jr. was inaugurated President in January 2001. His anti-China rhetoric during the campaign and the early part of the presidency included comments such as: "no strategic ambiguity: US will defend Taiwan against China", "China is a competitor, not a friend",[29] "do whatever it takes to defend Taiwan, including military action". After September 11, however, Bush reversed his position, apparently on the basis that the US could only afford conflict with one major adversary at a time. Collaboration arrangements on anti-terrorism and North Korea, amongst others, were finalised when Bush visited China in Feb 2002.[30] This was followed by the US-initiated the US–China Strategic Economic Dialogue (SED) in 2006. It took Bush Jr. 10 months to reverse his stance, a process that may have been expedited by September 11, but which would – given previous history – likely have happened to a greater or lesser degree even without this contributing factor.

It is not clear, however, that this trend will persist in the future. If presidents were previously free to use China as a rhetorical punching bag during their campaigns while quietly walking back their positions once in office, it was because China was generally a second- or third-order issue in the eyes of the media and the electorate. There was little concern that belligerent speeches would have significant consequences, and little condemnation of (or even interest in) the subsequent U-turns. The growing importance of China has made the old pattern harder to follow.

Thus, Obama began his term in a conciliatory position, describing China as a strategic partner, before bewildering and irritating all Asian powers with the clumsily-handled "pivot to Asia". By contrast, while Trump followed the pattern of being more aggressive at the beginning of his term and more conciliatory later on, this appears to have been part of a conscious negotiating strategy aimed at lowering tariffs, rather than campaign exuberance followed by a reluctant embrace of realism.[31]

Notes

1 Walter Russell Mead (2002). *Special Providence: American Foreign Policy and How It Changed the World*. New York: Routledge.

2 Perry Anderson (2015). *American Foreign Policy and Its Thinkers*. New York: Verso.

3 Perry Anderson (2015). *American Foreign Policy and Its Thinkers*. New York: Verso.

4 Walter A. McDougall (2016). *The Tragedy of US Foreign Policy: How America's Civil Religion Betrayed the National Interest*. New Haven, CT: Yale University Press.

5 Andrew Preston (2012). *Sword of the Spirit, Shield of Faith: Religion in American War and Diplomacy*. New York: Anchor Books. Yu Ge (2015). *The Essence of America* [美国的本质]. Beijing: Contemporary China Publishing House [当代中国出版社].

6 Tony Smith (2017). *Why Wilson Matters: The Origins of American Liberal Internationalism and Its Crisis Today.* Princeton, NJ: Princeton University Press.
7 Michael H. Hunt (1989). *Ideology and US Foreign Policy.* New Haven, CT: Yale University Press.
8 John G. Stoessinger (1985). *Crusaders and Pragmatists: Movers of Modern American Foreign Policy.* New York: W. W. Norton & Company.
9 Colin Dueck (2006). *Reluctant Crusaders: Power, Culture and Change in American Grand Strategy.* Princeton, NJ: Princeton University Press.
10 Stephen M. Walt (2006). *Taming American Power: The Global Response to US Primacy.* New York: W. W. Norton & Company: pp. 245–247.
11 Cecil V. Crabb Jr. (1985). *The American Approach to Foreign Policy: A Pragmatic Perspective.* London: University Press of America. Cecil V. Crabb Jr. (1989). *American Diplomacy and the Pragmatic Tradition.* London: Louisiana State University Press.
12 Paul R. Pillar (2016). *Why America Misunderstands the World: National Experience and Roots of Misperception.* New York: Columbia University Press.
13 Yu Huaiyan (2015). *Unfolding America: Pragmatism and Three Hundred Years of America* [深层美国：实用主义与美国的300年]. Beijing: Youyi Press [北京：中国友谊出版公司].
14 Joseph S. Nye Jr. (2004). *Soft Power: The Means to Success in World Politics.* New York: Public Affairs. Richard L. Armitage and Joseph S. Nye Jr. (2007). *A Smarter, More Secure America: A Report of the CSIS Commission on Smart Power.* Washington, DC: CSIS.
15 Ionut C. Popescu (2018). "Grand Strategy vs. Emergent Strategy in the Conduct of Foreign Policy." *Journal of Strategic Studies*, Vol. 41, No. 3, pp. 438–460. Hal Brands (2014). *What Good Is Strategy: Power and Purpose in American Statecraft from Harry S. Truman to George W. Bush.* Ithaca, NY: Cornell University Press.
16 Alexander Wendt (1992). "Anarchy Is What States Make of It: The Social Construction of Power Politics." *International Organization*, Vol. 46, No. 2, pp. 391–425.
17 William C. Martel (2015). *Grand Strategy in the Theory and Practice: The Need for an Effective American Foreign Policy.* New York: Cambridge University Press.
18 Christopher Layne (2006). *The Peace of Illusions: American Grand Strategy from 1940 to the Present.* Ithaca, NY: Cornell University Press.
19 Christopher Hemmer (2015). *American Pendulum: Recurring Debates in US Grand Strategy.* Ithaca, NY: Cornell University Press.
20 Robert Garson (1997). "Lyndon B. Johnson and the China Enigma." *Journal of Contemporary History*, Vol. 32, No. 1, pp. 63–80.
21 Steven I. Levine (1978). "China Policy During Carter's Year One." *Asian Survey*, Vol. 18, No. 5, pp. 437–447.
22 Ma Shikun (2015). "Why President Carter Is Popular in China." *China US Focus*, 18 November 2015. Accessed from: www.chinausfocus.com/culture-history/why-president-carter-is-popular-in-china. Accessed on 31 December 2017.
23 State Department. "The August 17 1982 US-China Communique on Arms Sales to Taiwan." Accessed from: https://history.state.gov/milestones/1981-1988/china-communique. Accessed on 31 December 2017.

24 Ronald Reagan (1984). "Remarks to Chinese Community Leaders in Beijing, China," 27 April 1984. Accessed from: www.presidency.ucsb.edu/ws/index.php?pid=39831. Accessed on 31 December 2017.
25 Indra De Soysa and Paul Midford (2012). "Enter the Dragon! An Empirical Analysis of Chinese Versus US Arms Transfers to Autocrats and Violators of Human Rights, 1989–2006." *International Studies Quarterly*, Vol. 56, No. 4, pp. 843–856.
26 Accessed from: www.hrw.org/legacy/campaigns/china-98/visit.htm. Accessed on 31 December 2017.
27 Accessed from: www.govtrack.us/congress/bills/106/hr4444. Accessed on 31 December 2017.
28 Bill Clinton (1996). *Between Hope and History*. New York: Penguin Random House: pp. 151–152.
29 New York Times, 26 February 2000, p. A10; GOP Debate on the Larry King Show, 15 February 2000; Inland Valley [So. Cal.] Daily Bulletin, 26 April 2001, p. 1. All quotes were extracted from: www.issues2000.org/celeb/George_W__Bush_China.htm. Accessed on 31 December 2017.
30 Transcript of President Bush's meeting with Jiang Zemin on 21 February 2002 in Beijing is self-explanatory on its positive vibes. Accessed from: https://2001-2009.state.gov/p/eap/rls/rm/2002/8564.htm. Accessed on 31 December 2017. China's equivalent archives is useful for comparison: www.china-embassy.org/eng/zmgx/zysj/bsfh/t36178.htm. Accessed on 31 December 2017.
31 Tom Phillips (2017). "Trump Praises China and Blames US for Trade Deficit." *The Guardian*, 9 November 2017. Accessed from: www.theguardian.com/world/2017/nov/09/donald-trump-china-act-faster-north-korea-threat. Accessed on 1 January 2018.

14 Small-P and Big-P pragmatism on the election trail

It is all very well to talk about dynamic equilibria and pendulum effects, but most general readers will find it hard to conceptualise such an abstract process without a few concrete examples. This chapter provides them. In it, we'll show how various presidents have – with many a noble phrase and an intransigent, aquiline stare – set out their ideological principles on the campaign trail, only to walk them back (or have them walked back by Congress and the judiciary) once in office.

While it is easy to be cynical about such flip-flopping, it should neverthe-less be contrasted with the alternative: a President who never compromises with the other branches of government, fighting tooth and nail to preserve ideological promises tossed to the crowds at ancient campaign meetings. A President who is too keen on compromise may be a weak individual, but he is seldom a danger to the Republic. The goal of the US check and balance system is not to ensure that manifesto promises are kept or to ensure that a strong leader rises to the top, but to contain the sort of rampaging narcissist who would willingly put themselves through the horrors of the campaign trail for a little worldly power. As such, while voters may despise the people making them, these compromises are not merely good, but central to the US democratic system. Indeed, part of the genius of modern US institutions can be said to lie in the way that they work to ensure that the aggregate of a million bad decisions is one good one.

The Nixon–Mao rapprochement: Seeing things from the other side

Having already covered this episode from the Chinese perspective, it is particularly instructive to return and turn upon it an American gaze.

The Johnson administration had, as described earlier, taken a relatively tough anti-China stance during the Vietnam War, without managing to alter the course of the conflict as a result. While a US rapprochement with

DOI: 10.4324/9781003202721-18

the People's Republic would be a practical way to reduce the communist threat in South East Asia while increasing the pressure on the Soviet Union, it could equally well be seen as the abandonment of an ally (Taiwan) in the pursuit of short-term gain. As early as 1967, Richard Nixon had already mentioned the idea of a rapprochement with red China, and his intent to ally with China against the Soviets, with Henry Kissinger originally disagreeing with the idea.[1] In fact, from the early days of the Long March until the advent of the Korean War, Mao had actually been keener to ally China with the US than with the Soviets. Nevertheless, by that point, the US had already hitched its wagon to the KMT star. When a series of Sino-Soviet skirmishes in the late 60's pushed Mao Zedong towards a closer relationship with the US, the US side jumped on the opportunity to reverse the previous administration's position without this being seen as a strategic loss or a public loss of face.[2] Kissinger contributed the idea of a strategic triangle to justify the policy, and to frame it in such a way as to make the apparent reversal more palatable to domestic opinion.[3] The new China policy was framed as a smart way to resolve the Vietnam issue, thus bringing a respectable end to a conflict that had become an albatross around the neck of the administration – an interesting and unusual example of an overtly pragmatic position appearing at the agenda-setting stage in US politics.[4]

Rapprochement was effectively a pragmatic partnership between two ideological opponents, each of which acknowledged that if the enemy of their enemy were not necessarily their friend, then he may at least be a useful partner. It can be seen as a repetition of Franklin Roosevelt's alliance with the USSR against the more pressing (at the time) Nazi threat. The stance accepted the possibility for co-existence between two contradictory ideological viewpoints, allowing the US and China to begin a series of bilateral cooperation arrangements. This rapprochement changed the strategic balance in the Cold War, helped the US to withdraw from Vietnam, divided the Socialist camp and pressured the Soviet Union. As such, the leadership judged that it was worth any loss in reputation concomitant to their edging away from their KMT allies, while nevertheless taking significant steps to frame the change in such a way as to minimise the damage to their image. Policymakers concluded that "improved Sino-American relations had caused the Soviets to feel less secure and made Moscow more willing to compromise with the Soviet Union over important issues as strategic arms limitation and disarmament in Europe".[5] Thus, we see the long-term pendulum swing in action, as an ill-advised policy becomes increasingly unpopular, forcing politicians to switch to a Big-P pragmatic national strategy for Small-P pragmatic electoral reasons.

Ronald Reagan and China's modernisation

Ronald Reagan's status as a pragmatic leader is not immediately apparent, thanks to his primary association with hard-line anti-communist stances, such as his famous "Evil Empire" speech.[6] Indeed, he is often cited as a great master of the use of hardline ideology as a campaign strategy – something that in itself should be considered an exercise of Small-P pragmatism. However, at least three aspects of Reagan's earlier foreign policies are noteworthy for their pragmatic characteristics:[7]

(1)   Reagan did not go so far as to associate China with the "Evil Empire", and in fact made provisions to reverse his earlier anti-China stance. Though he beat Carter in 1980 on an anti-China ticket. While the normalisation agreements had left the terms surrounding arms sales to Taiwan vague in order to allow Carter and Deng to defer a final decision to a later date, Congress passed the Taiwan Relations Act shortly afterwards which provided for continued arms sales in the future. Reagan himself was keen on the sale of FX fighters to Taiwan[8] which sparked off a crisis that was only alleviated by the August 1982 US–China Joint Communique, in which the US once more vaguely agreed to limit arms sales to Taiwan, and China agreed to seek a "peaceful solution" to the situation. The US finally settled for upgrading Taiwan's existing aircraft in a compromise option, on the basis that this would not – per Carter and Deng's agreement – qualitatively increase Taiwanese airpower against China. The 1982 US–China Communiqué on Arms Sales to Taiwan was another example of both US and Chinese pragmatism, incorporating pluralistic means, compromise and ambiguity.[9] Reaching an accord with China meant that Kissinger's "strategic triangle" strategy of isolating the Soviet Union could continue. James Mann surmised the underlying pragmatic reasoning: "Each side had probed the other's limits to the point of exhaustion. Both recognised, despite their differences, they had a great deal to offer one another. Both remained wary of Soviet's military power and intentions. China wanted American technology; America wanted its old dream of selling to the China market".[10]

(2)   Similarly, despite hard-line rhetoric, Reagan was also willing to collaborate with Mikhail Gorbachev in aiding the Soviet Union to liberalise itself both economically and politically.[11] Once again, however, the success of this strategy was dependent on the presence of a receptive leader on the other side to engineer the ideational conversion with respect to *glasnost* and *perestroika*.

(3)   Reagan also recognised in his policy-making by the weight of Congress, and devoted much time to garnering domestic support for his strategy. Reagan personally met 467 out of 535 members of Congress in his first 100 days.[12]

Indeed, Reagan can be considered in many ways to exemplify the phenomena associated with US pragmatism, with his clear swing from Small-P pragmatism during the agenda-setting stage, to Big-P pragmatism during the policy formulation and implementation stages, impelled by the weight of the forthcoming evaluation stage at the ballot box.

The Enemy of My Enemy: George Bush Jr. reconciles with China

In the early days of his campaign, George Bush Jr. pursued an 'anything but Clinton' strategy. As described earlier, this tendency for candidates to repudiate anything and everything endorsed by their predecessors is a common one. In Bush's case, this included a rejection of Clinton's newly accommodating China policy.

While Clinton and Jiang Zemin eventually managed to reach a 'Sino-US constructive partnership', this was rejected outright by the Bush campaign. Campaign literature described China as a 'strategic competitor of the United States' and the 'key challenge of the United States in Asia'. Bush also repeatedly accused Clinton of having devalued Japan, a long-standing ally in the Asia-Pacific region.[13] In the days immediately following his election, Bush stuck to his guns on the China issue, insisting that the US would help defend Taiwan in the event of a Chinese attack, and concluding a series of weapons and defence-related agreements with the Taiwanese government.[14]

To a large degree, the Bush administration was a war presidency in search of an enemy, and while China served the role admirably in the early years, following the September 11th attacks, it was immediately supplanted by a better candidate. Islamist terrorism fills all the unifying symbolic functions required of a national adversary, without – unlike China – having the potential to pose an existential threat.[15] Nevertheless, even prior to September 11th, it appeared that the administration was wary of pushing the rivalry with China into an outright conflict. After the April 2001 Hainan incident, in which a United States Navy EP-3E ARIES II signals intelligence aircraft and a People's Liberation Army Navy J-8II interceptor fighter jet collided, both sides made considerable efforts to downplay the significance of the episode.[16]

This tendency was compounded as the 'War on Terror' kicked into full gear. In the immediate aftermath of the initial attacks, the President made two goodwill visits to China, with Secretary of Defence Paul Wolfowitz now declaring that 'does not support Taiwan independence and has no intention to separate Taiwan from mainland China'. The visits were followed up with a series of high-level meetings in both China and the US, focusing principally on anti-terrorism policies. While the Chinese side was firmly opposed to US intervention abroad, it was nevertheless broadly aligned with the idea of a strong anti-terror policy, given the threats that it faced from its own internal minorities. Moreover, unlike other anti-war powers, Chinese opposition was relatively low-key and un-emphatic.

While the War on Terror has not gone down in history as an example of acute *realpolitick*, from the US perspective, the prospect of fighting a cold war with China at the same time as prosecuting hot wars in Afghanistan and Iraq did not appear practicable. Instead, US-China relations entered into a 'seven-year period of stability', covering the entirety of the rest of the Bush presidency.[17] This can largely be attributed to the pragmatic policy reversals made in the run-up to war.

Pragmatism in 21st-century America

Barack Obama and Donald Trump both served to exemplify the ways in which the US system compels its actors to be pragmatic, albeit in different ways.

While Barack Obama came to power on a moderate liberal platform, he was also extremely aware that he had won the votes of a substantial tranche of blue voters who had been pushed towards the Democrats more out of a dislike of the Republican party than because they were necessarily convinced by democratic policies. The result was that any policies that would be liable to be seen as "too left wing" would have been a bigger electoral risk for him than for a less avowedly centrist president. Thus, while Obama came to power on a relatively pacifist ticket – promising to close Guantanamo Bay, reduce the US's nuclear stockpile, and take a less overtly aggressive stance than his predecessor. In practice, however, the administration felt that any move towards enacting such policies would have opened him up to allegations of being weak on foreign policy, and the perceived precarity of his leadership increased the administration's to seize any wins it could. Thus, for example, the New START treaty was carefully crafted to allow both parties to actually increase the number of warheads that could be deployed (Russia's goal) while claiming to have reduced the overall number of missiles (the US goal) – the first of many instances of privileging appearances over reality. Similar perceptions of the electoral consequences of closing Guantanamo Bay and failing to intervene in Middle Eastern conflicts drove a foreign policy that was, by and large, as aggressive as that of the previous administration, though described in sunnier and more media-friendly terms. Conversely, the "pivot to Asia" was a strategy that appeared to be indicated as necessary by the circumstances, but which attracted almost no interest domestically. The result was a series of announcements that served mainly to worry China, while actual policy change rapidly lost momentum and fizzled out, largely because pursuing it doggedly would have borne few or no electoral benefits.

The Trump administration, on the other hand, was less preoccupied with small shifts in the polling needle, but had to contend with determined opposition on the part of Congress (occasionally) and the foreign policy establishment (always). The result was that while Trump managed to avoid starting any additional wars, attempts to remove troops from existing conflicts and reduce deployments in allied nations were regularly frustrated by internal opposition.

In each case, the President can be said to have been compelled to moderate his preferences and take a more pragmatic position in the system in which he was operating. In the first case, however, the driving force was direct electoral pressure, while in the second case, it was due to the pressure exerted by other political actors. In both cases, however, the result was the same: the president was dragged back towards a position that was closer to the "average" one held by all the actors rather than simply following his own inclinations.

Notes

1 The first evidence was Nixon's article in Foreign Affairs; this is corroborated with Singapore's Lee Kuan Yew who spoke to Nixon in 1967: 'we discussed the Vietnam War. But his main interest was China and what should US policy be'. Richard M. Nixon (1967). "Asia After Vietnam." *Foreign Affairs*, Vol. 46, October, p. 121. Lee Kuan Yew, Speech to Nixon Center for Peace and Freedom, Washington, DC, 11 November 1996. James Mann (2000). *About Face: A History of America's Curious Relationship with China, from Nixon to Clinton*. New York: Vintage Books: pp. 18–19. See also Walters who was army attache in US embassy in Paris who interacted with President Nixon on this issue. Vernon A. Walters (1978). *Silent Missions*. New York: Doubleday & Co: p. 257.
2 Roger Morris (1977). *Uncertain Greatness*. New York: Harper & Row, pp. 205–207. Walter Issacson (2005). *Kissinger: A Biography*. New York: Simon & Schuster: p. 353.
3 Walter Issacson (2005). *Kissinger: A Biography*. New York: Simon & Schuster: p. 336.
4 Greg Grandin (2015). *Kissinger's Shadow: The Long Reach of America's Most Controversial Statesman*. New York: Picador: p. 190.
5 Robert G. Sutter (1983). *The China Quandary: Domestic Determinants of US China Policy, 1972–1982*. Boulder, CO: Westview Press: pp. 54–55. See

also discussions in US Congress, House Committee on International Relations (1977). *United States-Soviet Union-China: The Great Power Triangle.* Washington, DC: US Government Printing Office.

6 Preston, Andrew (2012). *Sword of the Spirit, Shield of Faith: Religion in American War and Diplomacy.* New York: Anchor Books: p. 585.

7 David Priess (2016). *The President's Book of Secrets: The Untold Story of Intelligence Briefings to America's Presidents.* New York: Public Affairs: pp. 161–162.

8 Janice M. Hinton (1982). *The Sale of FX Aircraft to Taiwan.* Santa Monica, CA: RAND Corp.

9 James Mann (2000). *About Face: A History of America's Curious Relationship with China, from Nixon to Clinton.* New York: Vintage Books: p. 127.

10 James Mann (2000). *About Face: A History of America's Curious Relationship with China, from Nixon to Clinton.* New York: Vintage Books: p. 127.

11 James A. Nathan and James K. Oliver (1994). *Foreign Policy Making and the American Political System.* Baltimore, MD: Johns Hopkins University Press: p. 67.

12 Neil MacNeil and Richard A. Baker (2013). *The American Senate: An Insider's History.* New York: Oxford University Press: p. 138.

13 Yu Wanli (2009). "Breaking the Cycle? Sino-US Relations Under George W. Bush Administration." In *China's Shift: Global Strategy of the Rising Power.* Tokyo, Japan: National Institute for Defense Studies: pp. 81–98.

14 Robert Sutter (2006). "The Taiwan Problem in the Second George W. Bush Administration – US Officials' Views and Their Implications for US Policy." *Journal of Contemporary China*, Vol. 15, No. 48, pp. 417–441.

15 Cui Zhiyuan (2005). "The Bush Doctrine and Neoconservatism: A Chinese Perspective." *Harvard International Journal*, Vol. 46, p. 403.

16 Shirley A. Kan et al. (2002). "China-US Aircraft Collision Incident of April 2001: Assessments and Policy Implications." In *CRS Report for Congress*: pp. 1–33. Washington, DC: Congressional Research Services.

17 Yu Wanli (2009). "Breaking the Cycle? Sino-US Relations Under George W. Bush Administration." In *China's Shift: Global Strategy of the Rising Power.* Tokyo, Japan: National Institute for Defense Studies.

15 How the emergent properties of the US system force unpragmatic actors to make pragmatic decisions

As described earlier, the tendency to swing from more ideological stances to more pragmatic ones and back again seems to be largely the product of internal political factors (though contingent circumstances do have a role to play as well). To the extent that taking a strong ideological position on foreign policy issues has traditionally been seen to play well with the electorate, the pendulum effect can be seen as being at least partially the product of cultural factors. These, in turn, were influenced by geography, which has historically played a major role in influencing US perceptions of themselves, whether in terms of American exceptionalism or frontier mentality.[1]

In this section, we argue that internal socio-political factors, rather than external context, have traditionally driven US foreign policy swings from pragmatism to ideology and back again. While international and regional-level analysis is useful for understanding the context of a foreign policy decision, outside factors do not generally affect actors' inherent propensity for pragmatism.

On their soapboxes: Small-P pragmatism on the campaign trail

The fact that presidents are expected to specialise in and have strong positions on foreign policy makes it one of the principal domains in which candidates need to compete and differentiate their "product".[2] In this case, the easiest way to stand out and appear to provide change is simply to express positions that are the opposite of those held by the incumbent. As shown earlier, presidents have tended to become more pro-China towards the end of their mandates, meaning that for a challenger, an obvious strategy is to be visibly anti-China, a strategy that will inevitably later be tempered by the realities of office. They effectively set an ideological agenda that inevitably has to be walked back during the policy-formulation and implementation stages of the process. During electoral campaigning, presidential

DOI: 10.4324/9781003202721-19

candidates are already asked for their views on various international and domestic (even hypothetical) policy issues and often make 'ill-considered commitments in the heat of a political battle'.[3] In the face of traditional and social media reporting, leaders are often expected to be 'tougher-than-thou' during campaigns against challengers: the 'incumbent is burdened by a record that is replete with compromises and at best only partial successes in achieving the administration's stated objectives. The challenger, with less foreign policy experience, often simply asserts a seemingly clearer and more principled line. George H. W. Bush's ABC (All but Clinton) promise is a case in point, but Bush Jr. is not alone. Prior policy often sets the stage for evaluation, but evaluation is often more of a wish-based than a fact-based analysis. US leaders, given their political electoral and campaigning systems, have a stronger propensity for short-term thinking and adversarial thinking than leaders in one-party or multiparty states (which tend to be the product of electoral systems which also favour coalition-building).

Checks and balances and emergent qualities

The tendency to compromise once in office is reinforced by the check and balance system – showing that it is effectively the evaluation stage of the policy process that compels politicians to take increasingly pragmatic approaches to policy-formulation and implementation during their time in office. While this is weaker on foreign policy issues than on purely domestic ones (particularly in recent years), Congress is still capable of functioning as a check on presidential foreign policy – if only via its members' access to mass media outlets in which to express their misgivings.[4]

While the executive is the final arbiter, Congress amalgamates public opinion from media, civil society, experts, corporate, and challenges the Executive. Although Presidents can resort to Executive Orders to circumvent Congress, it is noteworthy that Congress (and particularly the Senate) can over-rule the President or at least led to legislative gridlock or filibuster.[5]

The State Department bureaucracy can often have a similar effect, with many of its members remaining in place from one administration to the next, they are ideally placed to minimise the effects of policies they dislike and pursue those that they favour, with or without the support of political blow-ins.[6]

Experts have traditionally been valued, and experts in think-tanks (independent and party-based) have influence on policy evaluation through their open-accessed products and actual advocacy. Moreover, US civil society and media are vibrant, given the constitutional protections for freedom of speech. While they do not have direct powers to change existing policies; their comments can have a strong influence on political decision-making.

The case of the Vietnam War illustrates the perpetual tension in the US system: "the paradox of Vietnam is that the foreign policy failed, but the domestic decision-making worked." The goal of containing communism was pursued consistently; elite and mass opinions were accommodated by compromise between extreme choices, satisfying partisans of neither extreme whilst preventing the total alienation of the other; and all views and recommendations were considered. Nevertheless, Leslie Gelb and Richard Betts conclude that "The system worked but yet it produced bad policy because it was a bad system".[7] On the plus side, however, the system also worked when "it facilitated decision-making on the means to end containment. keep costs of commitment as low as possible".[8] Similarly, the existence of competing centres of power allowed for the greater sharing of responsibility which aided US extrication from Vietnam because the political costs attached to policy reversal were shared by more actors.[9] While the system did eventually correct its actors' mistakes, it could not pre-empt bad decision-making entirely.[10]

Gelb and Betts describe Vietnam in broad terms as a failure of pragmatism (or as Gelb put it, "good old American common sense").[11] As Fareed Zakaria summarised the argument: "the true lesson of Vietnam is that allowing broad conceptual frameworks – global anti-communism, the domino theory- to dominate policy is a mistake, trapping policymakers into a rigid framework that forces action".[12]

The result is that "the United States is unilateral when it wants to be, multilateral when it must be".[13] Candidates running for office produce manifestos which tend to be policy wish lists rather than minimum viable products, with the desired policies gradually falling victim to countervailing forces from both inside and outside. From a Constitutional point of view this tendency towards long-run compromise is a bug rather than a feature, working to limit bad policy-making by excessively powerful presidents to as great a degree as possible (though recent experience shows that even the founding fathers could not entirely prevent this).[14] However, it also poses an external risk when allies and adversaries abroad come to see the US as a fundamentally unstable and unpredictable entity, whose commitments last – at best – only as long as the next electoral cycle.

US foreign policy as a product of the electoral system

In this chapter we have shown that US politicians – much like their Chinese counterparts – tend to be driven primarily by Small-P pragmatism, performing ideology on the campaign trail (at the agenda-setting stage) insofar as that it is required to ensure their political survival. Nevertheless, the

US electorate's ability to "kick the rascals out" every few years obliges leaders to become more Big-P pragmatic once in power, in order to provide the positive outcomes upon which they will be judged during the next electoral cycle. Thus the realities of the evaluation stage of the policy process compel pragmatism at the policy-formulation and implementation stages.

While systemic, cultural and contingent factors, as well as individual leadership styles, all interact in producing particularly policy orientations we would argue that the key to US pragmatism lies in domestic socio-political factors. International and regional contingencies should be regarded as background factors, while geographical and historical factors cannot be conclusively tied to any particular policy outcomes, given the proliferation of counterfactual arguments. In contrast, the meeting of domestic public opinion and foreign pressure as mediated via the electoral system are immediately visible and have been amply described, both in this paper and elsewhere.

The US political system was designed from the beginning to constrain potentially tyrannical leaders. While this is an effective means of preserving domestic stability, it can be both an advantage and a disadvantage in foreign policy-making. A strict constitutionalist would tend to argue that if the checks and balances system makes foreign policy difficult to implement, it is with the goal of discourage presidents from using it at all. In practice, however, the system has just as frequently led to foreign policy decisions that are failures precisely because they must please every veto-player in a system that was specifically designed to be staffed with them. The result is that fast and decisive action is often impossible, and foreign policy becomes a "horse designed by a committee", which in trying to satisfy everyone ends up satisfying no-one.

The phenomenon can be seen in the long series of drawn-out wars in recent years, where a desire to fulfil the goals of multiple constituencies – promotion of US values, casualty minimisation, resource economy, electoral gains, economic benefit – has led to an inability to set clear goals or to achieve the nebulous objectives assigned. Nevertheless, it can be said that though the mills of checks and balances may grind slowly, they grind exceeding small. The combination of external pressures abroad and the checks and balances system at home have eventually worked to correct these policies, as their failure becomes increasingly apparent at home and politicians promising a more isolationist stance grow increasingly popular.

Notes

1 Robert D. Kaplan (2017). *Earning the Rockies: How Geography Shapes America's Role in the World*. New York: Random House: p. 16.

2 Bruce Cronin (2001). "The Paradox of Hegemony: America's Ambiguous Relationship with the United Nations." *European Journal of International Relations,* Vol. 7, No. 1, pp. 103–130.

3 Kurt M. Campbell and James M. Steinberg (2008). *Difficult Transitions: Foreign Policy Troubles at the Outset of Presidential Power.* Washington, DC: Brookings Institution Press: p. 130.

4 Nathan and Oliver, 1994: pp. 72–90. Elaine C. Kamarck (2016). *Why Presidents Fail and How They Can Succeed Again.* Washington, DC: Brookings Institution Press: p. 152.

5 MacNeil and Baker, 2013: pp. 301–334.

6 Eugene R. Wittkopf and James M. McCormick (Eds.) (2008). *The Domestic Sources of American Foreign Policy: Insights and Evidence.* Lanham, MD: Rowman & Littlefield.

7 Leslie H. Gelb and Richard K. Betts (2016). *The Irony of Vietnam: The System Worked.* Washington, DC: Brookings Institution Press, reprint from 1979 edition: pp. 2–4.

8 Leslie H. Gelb and Richard K. Betts (2016). *The Irony of Vietnam: The System Worked.* Washington, DC: Brookings Institution Press, reprint from 1979 edition: p. 332.

9 Leslie H. Gelb and Richard K. Betts (2016). *The Irony of Vietnam: The System Worked.* Washington, DC: Brookings Institution Press, reprint from 1979 edition.

10 Leslie H. Gelb and Richard K. Betts (2016) *The Irony of Vietnam: The System Worked.* Washington, DC: Brookings Institution Press, reprint from 1979 edition: p. 2.

11 Leslie H. Gelb and Richard K. Betts (2016). *The Irony of Vietnam: The System Worked.* Washington, DC: Brookings Institution Press, reprint from 1979 edition.

12 Leslie H. Gelb and Richard K. Betts (2016). *The Irony of Vietnam: The System Worked.* Washington, DC: Brookings Institution Press, reprint from 1979 edition: p. XII.

13 David M. Malone and Yuen Foong Khong (Eds.) (2003). *Unilateralism & US Foreign Policy: International Perspectives.* Boulder, CO: Lynne Rienner: p. 375.

14 Richard Haass (2013). *Foreign Policy Begins at Home: The Case for Putting America's House in Order.* New York: Basic Books: p. 7.

Part V

What have we Learnt?

16 Varieties of pragmatism
Muddling through, in style

The aim of this book was to contribute to the devising of a conceptual framework that – firstly – fuses international relations and public policy definitions of pragmatism; secondly, derives a foreign policy-based model that, in a holistic manner, accounts for contextual and agential factors discussed in existing literature on the topic of pragmatism; and, thirdly, operationalises pragmatism in relation to specific details of the policy process in a way that will be useful to academics and practitioners alike.

The goal was then to use this framework in the context of rich, descriptive cases taken from the recent history of the US, China and Singapore. In doing this we hoped to demonstrate the utility of the conceptual framework (the three models of pragmatism in foreign policy), and to provide illustrations of the ways in which past policymakers have utilised pragmatism in the conduct of foreign affairs. At the same time, we aimed to evaluate the influence of different contextual and process factors on the three 'varieties of pragmatism', showing that while the situation of each state was different, they were nevertheless able to produce similar pragmatic outcomes.[1]

In this concluding summary we will explore in depth the differences and similarities between the varieties of pragmatism embraced by the US, China and Singapore. This conclusion, therefore, aims to provide relevant comparative observations from the three country-cases, to explore the ways in which they shed light on the pragmatism concept more generally, and to suggest certain avenues for future research.

In it, we will focus on the ways in which Small and Big-P pragmatism may interact in various political and institutional contexts, with each interaction being the product of a particular set of historical, geographical, social and political circumstances. We show that pragmatism can only be analysed effectively at the decision level, since the same individuals may adopt pragmatic and non-pragmatic positions at different stages of the policy process, depending upon the pressures to which they are subject.

DOI: 10.4324/9781003202721-21

Redefining pragmatism

The aim of this study was to look at a variety of different definitions of pragmatism emerging from philosophical, policy and popular literature, and to use a succession of country studies to attempt to isolate core and accessory components of the concept.

In practice, we found that no political system is consistently pragmatic or non-pragmatic. Instead, individual actors tend to move towards or away from pragmatic stances. The precise manner in which this happens is strongly influenced by domestic institutions and political culture. Interestingly, we have discovered that the principle dichotomy involved is often not pragmatism versus ideology, but rather Small-P pragmatism versus Big-P pragmatism. Thus, in the U.S. example, the pendulum swings tend to happen in the context of electoral battles. Candidates have greater freedom to act than incumbents, and a desire to adopt hard-line positions to appear strong and distinguish themselves from the compromises made by their predecessor as an inevitable part of holding office – a manifestation of Small-P pragmatism, given their frequent willingness to abandon these positions later. Once a candidate takes office, he finds himself forced to compromise with other actors (both internal and external) and make concessions, effectively being pushed into a Big-P pragmatic stance. In China, by contrast, the swing from Small-P to Big-P pragmatism tends to be – at least partially – a reflection of the level of security felt by the senior leader. A leader who is subject to internal challenges or forced to deal with rival power blocks is limited in his ability to take an individual position, and must compromise with other actors within the system to maximise the size of his own faction. In practice, this tends to involve a Small-P pragmatic willingness to perform ideological dogmatism to reassure others of in-group loyalty. Examples of this would include Deng Xiaoping during the early years of his time in power, or Hu Jintao. Stronger leaders have more latitude to act independently, though whether this leeway is used in pragmatic or ideological ways depends heavily upon the character of the individual. Thus, when Mao Zedong found himself in a position of strength, he took advantage of the fact to take a more ideological line, while Deng Xiaoping used the opportunity to pursue pragmatic policies at a faster rate than had previously been the case.

In Singapore, by contrast, existing evidence suggests that pragmatism (of the Big-P variety) that was once the fruit of a struggle for survival gradually comes – as a result of its own success – to become an ideology in itself, creating a tendency among bureaucrats to slide into group-think that pays lip-service to the concept and/or justify policy stagnation. Hope is not lost, however: as in China, the fact that the same party and individuals remain in power for a long time can help to align Big-P and Small-P pragmatism, and move towards systematising Strategic Pragmatism. Since both the party and its members will have to live with the consequences of their choices to a far greater degree than in other systems with higher political turnover, they have a stronger incentive to achieve solid, long-term results. This means that a Big-P pragmatic decision that achieves positive outcomes for the state is often also a Small-P pragmatic decision that improves the career prospects of those who made it. With political longevity, Singapore has had the conditions to think long term and systemically, and pragmatically implement their strategy, which are ingredients of Strategic Pragmatism. This means that while Singapore and Chinese leaders are capable of taking strategically pragmatic decisions, the same cannot be said of US Presidents, who are disincentivised from thinking more than eight years ahead.

Thus, while pragmatism is a common approach to policy-making, the causes behind its adoption may vary wildly. Adopting John S. Mill's method of difference, it is possible to isolate the effects of process factors. Thus, personalities of leaders and other policy agents matter most in foreign policy design and formulation in non-pluralistic political systems. China, for example, made a dramatic transition from ideological to pragmatic state over the course of just a few years following the death of Mao Zedong.

However, agency does not operate in a vacuum. Leaders' personalities are influenced by context: not just their individual history, but the broader context of international, regional and national happenings that affect their worldview. Geography (and notably whether their native country is a small or a big one) will also affect how agents view the role of their state in the global stage. For small states, every small issue is a big issue and international law is embraced dearly as a talisman against bigger states. The propagation of ideas and standard operating procedures within a given political system – largely as a product of historical factors – can also have a significant impact. Ideas can be institutionalised or even ossified into the social fabric. Thus, pragmatism or ideological behaviour can be less a conscious choice, and more a default reaction. This is tied to the ways in which given agents operate within the political system. In a non-pluralistic political system, it is most likely that the dominant personalities' worldviews and decisions will determine outcomes. In more pluralistic political systems (like the US), where there may be more than one centre of power, every decision is the product of the competing influences of multiple (or even millions of) individuals. Under such a system pragmatic decision-making is less likely to be an individual, top-down decision, and more likely to be the result of compromise across many viewpoints.

The Singapore example showed that highly vulnerable states are under more pressure to be pragmatic. For small states, regardless of political system, the more urgent pressure from outside and the lower degree of latitude enjoyed by decision-makers favours pragmatic decision-making as a way to remain abreast of external contingencies. Moreover, being small provides the advantage of relatively easy central control, and tight feedback loops. Hence, not only do small states show a greater propensity towards pragmatism out of a desire for survival, but they also find it easier to implement pragmatic policy-making and refine along the way.

As a result, it is generally more intellectually interesting to research the pragmatism of big states, since this requires more explanation than in the case of the small states described earlier. In this book we demonstrated that even in large states, pragmatic policy-making tends to be accompanied by a sense of existential anxiety or pressure from other actors. When leaders do not feel themselves to be under particular pressure, they are more likely to indulge in ideological behaviour. Thus, US presidential candidates – who as yet have no political responsibilities – tend to be ideological on the campaign trail but more pragmatic once in office. Similarly, Mao Zedong could not have taken power without a pragmatic approach to strategy, but once secured in his position was able to indulge ideological sentiments. This suggests that despite innate differences, countries as disparate as US and China may actually be more similar than conventionally thought.

The nature and paradox of pragmatism

Over the course of this book, we have looked at various perspectives on and facets of pragmatism, teasing out the real-world implications of each. Taking the idea of "strategic pragmatism" as the gold standard, we used this to situate different varieties of pragmatism along a continuum. Pragmatism and non-pragmatism are not binary values, but rather are situated at opposite ends of a sliding scale, with strategic pragmatism being the pinnacle. Similarly, one may distinguish between "Small-P" and "Big-P" pragmatism. In "Small-P" pragmatism, one behaves pragmatically for sub-national reasons (e.g. personal, party survival), and makes decisions based on sub-national interests, which may or may not produce pragmatic decisions at the national level. Thus, while Nixon-Mao rapprochement was strategic and ground-breaking in the 1970s, one could argue that it was a product of sub-national ("Small-P" pragmatic) impetus: to get China on-side in order to pave road for a US withdrawal from Vietnam and get Nixon re-elected. While this may have been in the long-run interests of the United States, this was arguably not the primary motivation for the decision, and the same decision may have been taken even had it not been in the national interest. One could further argue that this sub-national reasoning explains the lukewarm US normalisation effort after Nixon's resignation (during the Gerald Ford years). There is some overlap between pragmatism and principled pragmatism, with both lying in the middle ground between strategic pragmatism and non-pragmatism. Moreover, it can often be difficult to distinguish between principles and mere political rhetoric.

While strategic pragmatism maintained in view of a long-term goal (as displayed by China in its various territorial conflicts) can be taken as an ideal type, other forms and manifestations of pragmatism exist, whether as a product of forced compromise, a reflection of internal incentives, or other factors. Similarly, pragmatism may be present to differing degrees at different stages in the policy process, so a policy may begin life as a pragmatic decision but be doctrinaire in its application, or vice versa. From this observation, we concluded that pragmatism should be understood as a skill and acumen rather than a form of knowledge, insofar as that it must be continuously practiced and maintained in reference to contingent circumstances. Indeed, when it becomes standard operating procedure or an article of faith, it risks becoming ossified and ceasing to evolve. In such circumstances, what remains is not true pragmatism, but an "ideology of pragmatism". This being so, it is often the case that pragmatism is an easier approach for politicians to adopt in more challenging circumstances – that is to say, when they have no other choice in the matter. When under less pressure from outside factors, the temptation to indulge in wishful or ideological thinking often results in less pragmatic policy-making. The same phenomenon exists at both the micro and macro levels: thus, individual politicians will tend to be more ideological when under less pressure to produce results (notably, in US politics, when they are arguing as a candidate rather than a leader), but countries as a whole will also tend to grow less pragmatic as they become richer and more successful. This results in periodic swings towards and away from pragmatic policy-making. A country in tough circumstances adopts pragmatic policy-making strategies to deal with them, becomes more successful as a result, has greater room to indulge itself in ideology, backslides, and returns to the original state of precariousness which was a spur to pragmatism in the first place.

The continuum can best be expressed by means of a table (see Table 16.1):

Strategic pragmatism is the alignment of long-term strategic vision, realistically devised on the basis of a maximising agency's ability to solve contingent problems, and oft-articulated in a set of principles or ideological statements, with flexibility in implementation, which includes tactical adjustments to policy reversals, in order to achieve short- and long-term goals. This is the gold standard for Pragmatism. For parsimony's sake, it can be summarised in terms of five key features:

Realistic analysis: fact-based analysis of reality; reality as it is, not as one wishes.

Duality: striving for policy innovation or hybrids; breaks the either/or construct, moving towards a both/and construct (duality) where co-existence, mutual wins are possible and desired. This combines principles and pragmatism. Fitzgerald aptly surmised the essence of duality: "The test of first-rate intelligence is the ability to hold two opposed in mind at the same time and still retain the ability to function."[2]

Grand strategy: having a grand strategy to achieve desired strategic vision. Grand strategy has to demonstrate foresight (scenario

Table 16.1 The pragmatism continuum

	Non-pragmatic	Pragmatic (Small-P)	Principled pragmatism (Big-P)	Strategic pragmatism
Analysis	Wish-based analysis	Fact-based analysis	Fact-based analysis	Fact-based analysis
Emphasis	Dualism with an emphasis on principle	Dualism with an emphasis on pragmatism	Duality – Principled with pragmatic execution	Duality – Principled with pragmatic execution
Strategy	No grand strategy even when expedient	No grand strategy	No grand strategy	Grand Strategy
Implementation	Fixed implementation	Flexible implementation	Flexible implementation	Flexible implementation
Application	Universalism	Contextualism	Contextualism	Contextualism
Example	Mao Zedong great leap forward, cultural revolution	Nixon rapprochement with China	Deng with US over Taiwan; One country two systems	Singapore–China relations

planning) and insight (systems thinking) in analysis, and long-term planning to achieve long-lasting goals. This is differentiating factor between Strategic Pragmatism and Pragmatism.

Flexibility in implementation: adopting an experimental, trial-and-error approach during implementation which acknowledges that the initial plan may not be perfect. This entails tactical adjustments, operational changes, strategic policy reversals and tight feedback loops. This is a response to the dynamism inherent in complex reality.

Contextualism: having a propensity to reject universal application of particular principles/ideology regardless of context. Having a sensitivity to context allows one to better solve problems in a systemic and long-lasting manner.

At the opposite end of the scale, non-pragmatism is directed by ideology: driven by wish-based analysis and with principle predominating over being realistic when the two enter into conflict.

Principled pragmatism

Following up on the previous points, at any given moment it is rare to find that any given decision is entirely pragmatic or entirely ideological. More often than not, decisions reflect some form of principled pragmatism. The variation lies mostly in the extent of the hybridisation (more principled yet still pragmatic OR more pragmatic yet still principled). The US provides many classic examples of this phenomenon. While authors may try to divide US foreign policy deciders into "crusaders" and pragmatists, in reality the fluid inter-relationship between principles and pragmatism is such that it tends to be held that it is in the US national interest to uphold the nation's ideals and principles on the global stage. Indeed, it is even possible to argue that the US emphasis on liberal democratic ideology throughout the Cold War was a pragmatic policy aimed at extending national soft power and thus helping to ensure national survival. In other words, defending one's principles can be regarded as pragmatic, if it serves to attract international support or galvanise domestic public opinion in the cause of national survival. Conversely, in the name of its national interests, the US has regularly been willing to bend its principles (human rights, free markets, liberal democracy . . .) to support nations perceived as key partners.

Pragmatism in sequence

It is very difficult to judge with any degree of certainty whether a particular decision was pragmatic or not, and a large part of this is due to the contingent nature of pragmatism. A decision that is pragmatic at a given time may be non-pragmatic at another. Moreover, one particular policy may begin as a pragmatic decision and then grow into an entrenched ideological belief. Alternatively, an ideologically-inspired policy may be implemented in a thoroughly pragmatic manner. For research purposes, policy-making may be split into three stages: analysis, formulation and implementation. Thus the problem analysis might be pragmatically derived, but the solution not designed pragmatically; similarly, a pragmatic solution might not be pragmatically implemented. Thus, one could argue that while Nixon's rapprochement with China was "Small-P" pragmatism in the first instance, its implementation was "Big-P" pragmatic. Anecdotal evidence suggests that pragmatic implementation is more common than pragmatic formulation and analysis. Pragmatic analysis and formulation pertain more to the cognitive realm, and hence data collection is liable to false reporting from past practitioners, whose goal is often more to protect their legacy than to provide a purely accurate account of historical events. Pragmatic or non-pragmatic implementation is more easily assessed from outside, as it involves externalising cognitive processes into tangible actions. Moreover, true pragmatism requires pragmatism at every stage in the policy process, from analysis to formulation to implementation. In order to meet the criteria for genuine pragmatism, policy analysis must be fact-based and contextual, formulation should take dualism into account, and implementation must be flexible. Should any part of the process be non-pragmatic, then the benefits of pragmatism may not appear.

Pragmatism ossified as an ideology

When pragmatism is treated not as a contextual skill, but as a universal attribute, it risks becoming ossified as an ideology in and of itself.[3] Trying to operationalise pragmatism as an article of faith tends to reduce the pragmatism of individual agents rather than increasing it. Thus a habit becomes a standard operating procedure, and eventually an institution. As an institution, pragmatism is 'taught' to every bureaucrat and over time it becomes more important for bureaucrats to be seen to be pragmatic than to actually be pragmatic. Over time paying lip service to the idea of pragmatism becomes more important than making pragmatic decisions. Pragmatism then becomes a marketing slogan or convenient justification of one's actions, rather than a necessary survival skill. While the 'ideology of pragmatism' concept was adapted from Tan (2012) on the Singapore case, there is scope to argue that it is a natural evolution in any bureaucratic system. A slide towards an 'ideology of pragmatism' is likely affect all countries in which pragmatism is held up as a virtue among officials, as a natural reflection of systemic ossification. The US is far less susceptible to this problem, given the way in which competition between parties prevents ideological stagnation. Similarly, China's personality-centric leadership reduces the risk of it occurring within the PRC system. The risk is highest in Singapore, with its technocratic leadership.

Just getting by: survival and pragmatism

Historically, pragmatism has often been the strategy adopted by governments operating in survival mode, making decisions from a position of vulnerability. When one is (or believes oneself to be) vulnerable, reasons to be pragmatic are more pressing, a fact which we took as the focus of first model. Conversely, when one is not in a position of vulnerability, pragmatism becomes a choice; other factors may weigh in more strongly – usually factors surrounding identity and ideology. This is especially the case for large and well-resourced states, which tend to enjoy more leeway in their actions than small and bereft ones. Singapore is a classic example of a small state that has adopted a siege mentality and continued to operate in survival mode even long after its geopolitical vulnerability receded. Singapore case found that geography was dominant contextual factor influencing Singapore's pragmatic behaviour. This being said, it is not inevitable that small and resource-deprived states will automatically exhibit pragmatic behaviour. Power structures and the individual psychology of the leaders also play a strong role. This explains why the first model helps to explain some incidences of pragmatic foreign policy making of small states, but not all. While Singapore was cited as the principal example of this, it is nevertheless worth remembering that Singapore is an exceptional case. The majority of states subject to equal or even greater pressure do not become pragmatic powerhouses in the Singapore manner. The mere presence of outside pressure is not a guarantee of pragmatic governance, and may be more likely to produce in-fighting, ideology, or domestic chaos.

This raises the question of states that lie somewhere in the middle, between small-and-poor and large-and-rich. How, for example, do large poor states behave? Are they more likely to adopt pragmatic or ideological policies? In fact, large poor states have a choice. They can afford to be un-pragmatic, having the option to settle for a less luxurious mode of survival if following ideological dictates so compels them. China during the Cultural Revolution can be seen as a good example of this. The county was large enough to survive the consequences of its non-pragmatism, but the effects of its preference for ideology are thrown into sharp relief when the period is contrasted with the (more pragmatic) Deng Xiaoping era that followed.

The shift between ideology and pragmatism can also operate in the opposite direction. Having grown successful through the application of pragmatic policies, countries may realise that they now have the leeway required to behave in un-pragmatic ways, whether by indulging in ideology almost in the manner of a luxury good (as in the case of the neoconservative US leadership in recent years, embarking on foreign wars largely for signalling purposes) or by transforming pragmatism itself into an ideology (see the "Ideology of Pragmatism" section given earlier).[4] Similarly, we mentioned the possibility of a similar effect taking hold in Singapore as it grows increasingly successful, with an "ideology of pragmatism" taking the place of genuine pragmatism as the government finds itself under less internal and external pressure.

Furthermore, following on from the above point, the drift from pragmatic to un-pragmatic policy-making or vice versa is not necessary a one-time-only event. The US and China have both demonstrated recurring swings between pragmatism and non-pragmatism. Just as pragmatic policies may produce enough leeway to allow leaders to behave un-pragmatically, by producing adverse effects sufficient to damage the national interest, un-pragmatic policies tend, in the long term, to place those who adopt them in a situation in which they will – sooner or later – be forced to adopt pragmatic positions or face the possibility of being wiped out. Thus, the damage done by the Great Leap Forward and Cultural Revolution had to be rectified by a suite of pragmatic policies introduced by Deng Xiaoping. It remains to be seen whether China will become un-pragmatic once more as it grows more successful.

Notes

1 Interview with Ezra Vogel, 17 May 2017.
2 F. Scott Fitzgerald (1925). *Great Gatsby*. New York: Charles Scribner's Sons.
3 Kenneth Paul Tan (2012). "The Ideology of Pragmatism: Neo-Liberal Globalisation and Political Authoritarianism in Singapore." *Journal of Contemporary Asia*, Vol. 42, No. 1, February, pp. 67–92.
4 Paul Kennedy (2010). *The Rise and Fall of the Great Powers*. London: Vintage Books.

17 Strategic and systemic pragmatism through dynamic equilibria . . .

"Is he lucky?"

– Cardinal Mazarin

Many analyses of political pragmatism – and particularly many of those covered in the Singapore section of the present book – tend to interpret pragmatism as a form of Aristotelian *phronesis*. It is seen as practical wisdom, whether expressed through the behaviour of an individual or a group. While this is a perfectly valid interpretation of the concept (and indeed, one that we happily endorse), its wider implications are few, simply because it is not a quality that may be induced or acquired by study. As Aristotle himself put it:

> [A]lthough the young may be experts in geometry and mathematics and similar branches of knowledge, we do not consider that a young man can have *phronesis*. The reason is that *phronesis* includes a knowledge of particular facts, and this is derived from experience, which a young man does not possess; for experience is the fruit of years.

While it is certainly a useful semantic distinction, from a systemic point of view it is rather like luck – one would certainly wish to have a leader who possesses it, but it is difficult or impossible to guarantee such an outcome.

There are certainly ways to try to create individuals who think pragmatically – the use of apprenticeship systems rather than standard operating procedures springs to mind, and the use of lateral thinking and systems approaches to problems – the complexity of the interactions between individuals and institutions means that there is no way to guarantee the presence of a pragmatic leader at the helm of any given country.

Simply put, there is no list of behaviours that can be followed to "do" pragmatism, simply because pragmatism is always a contingent quality.

DOI: 10.4324/9781003202721-22

Instead, it has to become an ingrained mode of being (acumen). Something of this can be observed in the Singapore case, wherein momentary responses to a situation gradually formed into preferences, which became habits, and then a self-reinforcing system.

What is more interesting, from a policy science perspective, is the idea of political systems that force actors to behave pragmatically, even when it is against their nature. While the Singapore system may one day become such, it has not yet had enough years to conclusively demonstrate it. But the longevity of Singapore's political system thus far does give it stability to think and plan long term, implement, adjust and reverse according to changes in reality, which are defining components of Strategic Pragmatism. On the other hand, it can be argued that the Chinese and US systems both aim for this in different ways, succeeding in some and failing in others. While the Chinese technocratic system has a power to moderate the positions of the top leadership, it can also produce runaway ideological purity spirals in which no one dares to challenge the party doctrine or the dominant leader. By contrast, the democratic competition in the US system forces politicians to find a compromise, but does so via a dynamic equilibrium process wherein a moderate outcome only in the midst of an unending series of swings towards the extremes. However, this does not constitute Strategic Pragmatism, as the decision horizon is never more than eight years ahead.

In writing this book, we hope that our analysis of this specific concept of strategic and systemic pragmatism will be of service to policymakers as they adapt and redesign institutions. For while pragmatism – like luck – cannot be programmed to appear within a state, circumstances may be created so as to allow a government to take maximum advantage of it when it does appear. Essentially, we need a policy hybrid of American systemic pragmatism through dynamic equilibria, with Singapore's long-term thinking and political longevity, Chinese patience and flexibility in implementation. A fusion of Eagle, Lion and Dragon: too tall an order?

Let's start small.

We humbly submit the following advice, culled from the cases under investigation in the present work:

1   Throw the rascals out . . .
    If politicians feel that they will be judged on the consequences of their policies, then this gives them an incentive to propose realistic policies, rather than merely barn-burning rhetoric.
2   . . . but not too often.
    On the other hand, when a politician knows that he will be out of office in a few years whatever happens, he has just as little incentive to worry about the consequences of his actions as if he were installed for life.

3   Make 'em fight . . .

The aggregate of a million bad decisions tends to be one good one. Forcing politicians to haggle for a mutually acceptable solution pushes them towards a more pragmatic (and innovative) frame of mind, wherein everyone can be a winner in a different 'currency'.

4   . . . but not too intensely.

When ideology comes to be seen as a question of moral purity, then negotiation becomes impossible. When we are good and they are evil, any attempt at compromise becomes an immoral act. Perceptions of the opposition cannot be so hardened that they do not allow participants to conceive that a win–win solution may be possible.

5   And finally, find a source of outside pressure.

When an existential external threat is present, whether natural or manmade, internal ideological become less important, and compromise becomes more likely, as a result of the need to deal with the outside pressure. Think: aliens, climate change . . .

This book concludes with the earnest hope that pragmatism as a problem-solving approach, skill, acumen and state of being can be more widely adopted and practised by practitioners, and further researched by academics worldwide. Our future generations are in urgent need of a more pragmatic world where complex policy problems as such as climate change and sustainability can be more pragmatically solved by stakeholders at different levels of governance, for long-term win–win outcomes.

Bibliography

Abadi, Jacob, 'Pragmatism and Rhetoric in Yemen's Policy Towards Israel', *Journal of Third World Studies*, Vol. 16, No. 2, Fall 1999, pp. 95–118.

Abadi, Jacob, 'Algeria's Policy Towards Israel: Pragmatism and Rhetoric', *Middle East Journal*, Vol. 56, No. 4, Autumn 2002, p. 616.

Acharya, Amitav (1998) *The Quest for World Order: Perspectives of a Pragmatic Idealist*, Singapore: Institute of Policy Studies and Times Academic Press.

Acharya, Amitav (2008) *Singapore's Foreign Policy: The Search for Regional Order*, Singapore: World Scientific.

Allison, Graham and Robert D. Blackwill with Ali Wyne (2012) *Lee Kuan Yew: The Grand Master's Insights on China, the United States, and the World*, Cambridge, MA: Massachusetts Institute of Technology Press.

Althaus, Catherine, Peter Bridgman and Glyn Davis (2013) *Australian Policy Handbook*, New South Wales: Allen and Unwin.

Amstutz, Mark R. (2014) *Evangelicals and American Foreign Policy*, New York: Oxford University Press.

Anderson, James E. (1975) *Public Policy Making*, New York: Praeger.

Anderson, Perry (2015) *American Foreign Policy and Its Thinkers*, New York: Verso.

Ang Chen Guan (2013) *Singapore, ASEAN and the Cambodian Conflict 1978–1991*, Singapore: NUS Press.

Armitage, Richard L. and Joseph S. Nye Jr. (2007) *A Smarter, More Secure America: A Report of the CSIS Commission on Smart Power*, Washington, DC: Center for Strategic and International Studies.

Austin, Ian Patrick (2004) *Goh Keng Swee and Southeast Asian Governance*, Singapore: Marshall Cavendish Academic.

Austin, Ian Patrick (2011) *Australia-Singapore Relations: Successful Bilateral Relations in a Historical and Contemporary Context*, Singapore: Select.

Baker, Jim (1991) *Crossroads: A Popular History of Malaysia and Singapore*, Singapore: Marshall Cavendish.

Baker, Jim (2005) *The Eagle in the Lion City: America, Americans and Singapore*, Singapore: Landmark.

Balakrishnan, Vivian. Transcript Remarks by Minister for Foreign Affairs Dr Vivian Balakrishnan at the MFA Townhall on 17 July 2017. Accessed from: www.mfa.gov.sg/content/mfa/media_centre/press_room/pr/2017/201707/press_2017071703.html. Accessed on 14 January 2018.

Barr, Michael D. (2000) *Lee Kuan Yew: The Beliefs Behind the Man*, Kuala Lumpur: New Asian Library.

Barr, Michael D. (2002) *Cultural Politics and Asian Values: The Tepid War*, Oxon: Routledge.

Barr, Michael D. (2014) *The Ruling Elite of Singapore: Networks of Power and Influence*, Bangkok: New Asian Library.

Bauer, Harry and Elisebetta Brighi (2009) *Pragmatism in International Relations*, Oxon: Routledge.

Baylis, John (1993) *The Diplomacy of Pragmatism: Britain and the Formation of NATO, 1942–49*, Basingstoke: Macmillan.

Beinhocker, Eric D. (2006) *The Origin of Wealth: Evolution, Complexity and the Radical Remaking of Economics*, Cambridge, MA: Harvard Business Review Press.

Bell, Daniel A. (2016) *The China Model: Political Meritocracy and the Limits of Democracy*, Princeton, NJ: Princeton University Press.

Bernstein, Richard, 'The Resurgence of American Pragmatism', *Social Research*, Vol. 59, 1992, pp. 813–840.

Bloodworth, Dennis (2011) *The Tiger and the Trojan Horse*, Singapore: Marshall Cavendish.

Borschberg, Peter (2010) *The Singapore and Melaka Straits: Violence, Security and Diplomacy in the 17th Century*, Singapore: NUS Press.

Bourgon, Jocelyne (2011) *A New Synthesis of Public Administration: Serving the 21st Century*, Montreal: McGill-Queen's University Press.

Bradley, James (2015) *The China Mirage: The Hidden History of American Disasters in Asia*, New York: Little, Brown & Co: pp. 311–312, 323.

Brands, Hal (2014) *What Good Is Strategy: Power and Purpose in American Statecraft from Harry S. Truman to George W. Bush*, Ithaca, NY: Cornell University Press.

Burke, F. Thomas (2013) *What Pragmatism Was*, Bloomington, IN: Indiana University Press: p. 148.

Bush, George W. (2010) *Decision Points*, New York: Crown Publishers.

Butler, Brian E. ' "Obama" Pragmatism in International Relations: Appropriate or Appropriation?' in Shane J. Ralston (Ed.) (2013), *Philosophical Pragmatism and International Relations: Essays for a Bold New World*, Plymouth: Lexington Books: pp. 159–176.

Calder, Kent E. (2017) *Singapore: Smart City Smart State*, Washington, DC: Brookings Institution Press.

Campbell, Kurt M. and James M. Steinberg (2008) *Difficult Transitions: Foreign Policy Troubles at the Outset of Presidential Power*, Washington, DC: Brookings Institution Press: p. 130.

Capra, Fritjof (1982) *The Turning Point: Science, Society and the Rising Culture*, New York: Simon & Schuster.

Capra, Fritjof and Pier Luigi Luisi (2014) *The Systems View of Life: A Unifying Vision*, New York: Cambridge University Press.

Chan Chun Sing. Speech at the 'Future China Global Forum and Singapore Regional Business Forum 2018', MTI, 28 August 2018. Accessed from: www.mti.gov.sg/Newsroom/Speeches/2018/08/Speech-by-Minister-Chan-Chun-Sing-at-the-CCI-STC-Seminar-2018. Accessed on 4 May 2019.

Chan Heng Chee. 'Politics in an Administrative State: Where has the Politics Gone?', Occasional Papers, No. 11, Department of Political Science, University of Singapore, 1975.

Chan Heng Chee (1976) *Dynamics of One Party Dominance*, Singapore: Singapore University Press.

Chan Heng Chee (1988) *Singapore: Domestic Structure and Foreign Policy: Final Draft*.

Chan Heng Chee and Obaid ul Haq (2007) *S. Rajaratnam: The Prophetic and the Political*, Singapore: ISEAS Press.

Chen Dunde (2014) *China-US Diplomatic Relationship Establishment: Documentary of the Handshake Between Deng Xiaoping and Carter* [中美建交: 邓小平与卡特握手纪实], Beijing: China Youth Press.

Chen Jian (2013) *Diplomacy Leads to World Harmony*, Beijing: Current Affairs Press.

Chen Jie (1992) *Ideology in US Foreign Policy: Case Studies in US China Policy*, Westport, CT: Praeger.

Chen Jie (2002) *Foreign Policy of the New Taiwan: Pragmatic Diplomacy in Southeast Asia*, Cheltenham: Edward Elgar.

Cheong Yong Mun (2004) *The Indonesian Revolution and the Singapore Connection: 1945–1949*, Singapore: NUS Press.

Chew, Emrys and Chong Guan Kwa (2012) *Goh Keng Swee: A Legacy of Public Service*, Singapore: World Scientific.

Chiang Hai Ding (2015) *Elections in Singapore 1948–2011*, Singapore: Straits Times Press.

Chiang Hai Ding and Rohan Kamis (2014) *We Also Served: Reflections of Singapore's Former PAP MPs*, Singapore: Straits Times Press.

Chin, James, 'Lee Kuan Yew and Malaysia', *The Roundtable*, Vol. 104, No. 3, 2015, p. 347.

Chin Kin Wah (1974) *The Five Power Defence Arrangements and AMDA*, Singapore: ISEAS Press.

China United Nations Association (2009) *China's UN Diplomacy* [中国联合国协会, 中国的联合国外交], Beijing: World Knowledge Press.

Ching, Frank, 'Pragmatism Is the Hallmark of Peking's Foreign Policy', *Far Eastern Economic Review*, 24 June 1993, p. 31.

Cho Il Hyun and Park Seo-Hyun, 'Anti-Chinese and Anti-Japanese Sentiments in East Asia: The Politics of Opinion, Distrust, and Prejudice', *The Chinese Journal of International Politics*, Vol. 4, No. 3, 2011, pp. 265–290.

Chong, Alan, 'Singapore Foreign Policy and Asian Values Debate: 1992–2000: Reflections on an Experiment on Soft Power', *The Pacific Review*, Vol. 17, No. 1, March 2004, pp. 95–133.

Chong, Alan, 'Singapore's Foreign Policy Beliefs as "Abridged Realism": Pragmatic and Liberal Prefixes in the Foreign Policy Thought of Rajaratnam, Lee, Koh and Mahbubani', *International Relations of the Asia Pacific*, Vol. 6, No. 2, August 2006, pp. 269–306.

Chong, Terence (2010) *Management of Success: Singapore Revisited*, Singapore: ISEAS Press.

Chua Beng Huat (1997) *Communitarian Ideology and Democracy in Singapore*, Oxon: Routledge.

Chua Beng Huat (2009) *Communitarian Politics in Asia*, Oxon: Routledge.

Chua Wei Boon, Daniel (2017) *US-Singapore Relations, 1965–1975*, Singapore: NUS Press.

Chung Chien-peng (2004) *Domestic Politics, International Bargaining and China's Territorial Disputes*, New York: Routledge.

Claude Jr., Inis L., 'The Tension Between Principle and Pragmatism in International Relations', *Review of International Studies*, Vol. 19, No. 3, July 1993, pp. 215–226.

Clinton, Bill (1996) *Between Hope and History*, New York: Penguin Random House.

Colander, David and Roland Kupers (2014) *Complexity and the Art of Public Policy: Solving Society's Problems from the Bottom-Up*, Princeton, NJ: Princeton University Press.

Cornell, Katherine F., 'From Patronage to Pragmatism: Central Europe and the United States', *World Policy Journal*, Vol. 13, Spring 1996, p. 91.

Cornell, Svante E., 'Iran and the Caucasus: The Triumph of Pragmatism Over Ideology', *Global Dialogue*, Vol. 3, Nos. 2–3, Spring 2001, p. 91.

Coufoudakis, Van, 'Ideology and Pragmatism in Greek Foreign Policy', *Current History*, Vol. 81, No. 479, December 1982, pp. 426–432.

Crabb Jr., Cecil V. (1985) *The American Approach to Foreign Policy: A Pragmatic Perspective*, London: University Press of America.

Crabb Jr., Cecil V. (1989) *American Diplomacy and the Pragmatic Tradition*, London: Louisiana State University Press.

Cronin, Bruce, 'The Paradox of Hegemony: America's Ambiguous Relationship with the United Nations', *European Journal of International Relations*, Vol. 7, No. 1, 2001.

Cui Zhiyuan, 'The Bush Doctrine and Neoconservatism: A Chinese Perspective', *Harvard International Journal*, Vol. 46, 2005.

Dagli, Murat, 'The Limits of Ottoman Pragmatism', *History and Theory*, Vol. 52, May 2013, pp. 202–203.

Darusman, Suryono (2000) *Singapore and the Indonesian Revolution 1945–1950: Recollections of Suryono Darusman*, Singapore: ISEAS Press.

Datta-Ray, Sunanda K. (2009) *Looking East to Look West: Lee Kuan Yew's Mission India*, Singapore: ISEAS Press.

Davis, Jonathan E., 'From Ideology to Pragmatism: China's Position on Humanitarian Intervention in the Post Cold War Era', *Vanderbilt Journal of Transnational Law*, Vol. 44, No. 2, March 2011, pp. 217–283.

Desker, Barry. 'Against All Odds: Singapore's Successful Lobbying on the Cambodia Issue at the United Nations', Occasional Paper, ISEAS Press, Singapore, 2016.

Desker, Barry and Ang Cheng Guan (2016) *Perspectives on Security of Singapore*, Singapore: World Scientific.

Desker, Barry and Chong Guan Kwa (2012) *A Public Career Remembered: Goh Keng Swee*, Singapore: World Scientific.

De Soysa, Indra and Paul Midford, 'Enter the Dragon! An Empirical Analysis of Chinese Versus US Arms Transfers to Autocrats and Violators of Human Rights, 1989–2006', *International Studies Quarterly*, Vol. 56, No. 4, 2012.

de Waal, Cornelis (2005) *On Pragmatism*, Belmont, CA: Wadsworth.

Dickstein, Morris (2005) *The Revival of Pragmatism*, Durham, NC: Duke University Press: p. 1.

Drysdale, John (2009) *Singapore: Struggle for Success*, Singapore: Marshall Cavendish.

Dueck, Colin (2006) *Reluctant Crusaders: Power, Culture and Change in American Grand Strategy*, Princeton, NJ: Princeton University Press.

Dueck, Colin (2010) *Hard Line: The Republican Party and US Foreign Policy Since World War II*, Princeton, NJ: Princeton University Press.

Duggan, William (2003) *The Art of What Works: How Success Really Happens*, New York: McGraw-Hill.

Engerman, David C., 'John Dewey and the Soviet Union: Pragmatism Meets Revolution', *Modern Intellectual History*, Vol. 3, No. 1, April 2006, pp. 35–36.

Farrell, Brian P. (2011) *Churchill and the Lion City: Shaping Modern Singapore*, Singapore: NUS Press.

Feinsilver, Julie M., 'Fifty Years of Cuba's Medical Diplomacy: From Idealism to Pragmatism', *Cuban Studies*, Vol. 41, 2010, p. 85.

Feng Zhang (2015) *Chinese Hegemony: Grand Strategy and International Institutions in East Asian History*, Redwood City, CA: Stanford University Press.

Festenstein, Matthew (1997) *Pragmatism and Political Theory*, Chicago, IL: University of Chicago Press: p. 2.

Folensbee, Fadhma Izri (2011) *Spreading Democracy: Supporting Dictators: Pragmatism and Ideology in US Foreign Policy in the Global War on Terror*, Saarbrucken: LAP Lambert Academic Publishing.

Freeman, Chas (2012) *Interesting Times*, Charlottesville, VA: Just World Books.

Friedberg, Aaron L. (2011) *A Contest for Supremacy: China, America, and the Struggle for Mastery in Asia*, New York: W. W. Norton & Company.

Friedrichs, Jorg and Friedrich Kratochwil, 'On Acting and Knowing: How Pragmatism Can Advance International Relations Research and Methodology', *International Organization*, Vol. 63, Fall 2009, pp. 701–731.

Frost, Mark and Yu-Mei Balasingamchow (2009) *Singapore: A Biography*, Singapore: EDM.

Fu Ying (2013) *A Voice from China: Selected Speeches of Fu Ying* [来自中国的声音: 傅莹大使演讲录], Hong Kong: Chung Hwa Books.

Ganesan, Narayanan (1989) *Singapore's Foreign Policy in ASEAN: Major Domestic and Bilateral Political Constraints*, DeKalb, IL: Northern Illinois University.

Ganesan, Narayanan (2005) *Realism and Interdependence in Singapore's Foreign Policy*, Oxon: Routledge.

Ganguly, Sumit, 'India's Foreign Policy Grows Up', *World Policy Journal*, Vol. 20, No. 4, Winter 2003–2004, pp. 44–45.

Gao Wenqian (2007) *Zhou Enlai: The Last Perfect Revolutionary*, New York: Public Affairs.

Gardini, Gian Luca and Peter Lambert (2011) *Latin American Foreign Policies: Between Ideology and Pragmatism*, New York: Palgrave Macmillan.

Garson, Robert, 'Lyndon B. Johnson and the China Enigma', *Journal of Contemporary History*, Vol. 32, No. 1, 1997.

Gelb, Leslie H. and Richard K. Betts (2016) *The Irony of Vietnam: The System Worked*, Washington, DC: Brookings Institution Press, reprint from 1979 edition.

Geyer, Robert and Paul Cairney (2015) *Handbook on Complexity and Public Policy*, Cheltenham: Edward Elgar.

Godwin, Jack (2008) *The Arrow and the Olive Branch: Practical Idealism in US Foreign Policy*, Westport, CT: Praeger.

Goh, Evelyn and Daniel Chua (2015) *Diplomacy*, Singapore: Straits Times Press.

Goldstein, Avery (2008) *Rising to the Challenge: China's Grand Strategy and International Security*, Singapore: NUS Press.

Goldstein, Judith and Robert O. Keohane (1993) *Ideas and Foreign Policy: Beliefs, Institutions, and Political Change*, Ithaca, NY: Cambridge University Press.

Gong Li (2016) *Peaceful Development: Interpreting China's Diplomatic Principles*, Beijing: Foreign Languages Press.

Grandin, Greg (2015) *Kissinger's Shadow: The Long Reach of America's Most Controversial Statesman*, New York: Picador.

Haass, Richard (2013) *Foreign Policy Begins at Home: The Case for Putting America's House in Order*, New York: Basic Books.

Hack, Karl and Kevin Blackburn (2005) *Did Singapore Have to Fall? Churchill and the Impregnable Fortress*, Oxon: Routledge.

Hack, Karl and Jean-Louis Margolin with Karine Delaye (2010) *Singapore from Temasek to the 21st Century: Reinventing the Global City*, Singapore: NUS Press.

Han Fook Kwang, Warren Fernandez and Sumiko Tan (1998) *Lee Kuan Yew: The Man and His Ideas*, Singapore: Straits Times Press.

Han Fook Kwang, Zuraidah Ibrahim, Chua Mui Hoong, Lydia Lim, Ignatius Low, Rachel Lin and Robin Chan (2011) *Lee Kuan Yew: Hard Truths to Keep Singapore Going*, Singapore: Straits Times Press.

Hays Gries, Peter (2014) *The Politics of American Foreign Policy: How Ideology Divides Liberals and Conservatives Over Foreign Affairs*, Redwood City, CA: Stanford University Press.

Heilmann, Sebastian and Elizabeth J. Perry (2011) *Mao's Invisible Hand: The Political Foundations of Adaptive Governance in China*, Cambridge, MA: Harvard University Press.

Hellman, Gunther, 'Beliefs as Rules for Action: Pragmatism as a Theory of Thought and Action', *International Studies Review*, Vol. 11, 2009, pp. 638–662.

Hemmer, Christopher (2015) *American Pendulum: Recurring Debates in US Grand Strategy*, Ithaca, NY: Cornell University Press.

Heng Derek, Kwa Chong Guan and Tan Tai Yong (2009) *Singapore, a 700 Year History: From Early Emporium to World City*, Singapore: National Archives Singapore.

Heng Swee Keat. Speech by Mr Heng Swee Keat, Minister for Education, at "The Big Ideas of Mr Lee Kuan Yew" Conference, on Monday, 16 September 2013, at 1.10pm, at The Shangri-La Hotel Singapore. Accessed from: www.moe.gov.sg/media/speeches/2013/09/16/speech-by-mr-heng-swee-keat-at-the-big-ideas-of-mr-lee-kuan-yew-conference.php. Accessed on 1 October 2013.

Hill, Michael and Lian Kwen Fee (1995) *The Politics of Nation Building and Citizenship in Singapore*, London: Routledge.

Hinton, Janice M. (1982) *The Sale of FX Aircraft to Taiwan*, Santa Monica, CA: RAND Corp.

Ho, Peter (2018) *The Challenges of Governance in a Complex World*, Singapore: World Scientific.

Homer-Dixon, Thomas (2002) *Ingenuity Gap – Facing the Economic, Environmental, and Other Challenges of an Increasingly Complex and Unpredictable Future*, New York: Vintage Books.

Hong, Lysa and Huang Jianli (2008) *The Scripting of a National History: Singapore and Its Pasts*, Singapore: NUS Press.

Ho Shu Huang and Samuel Chan (2015) *Defence*, Singapore: Straits Times Press.

House Committee on International Relations (1977) *United States-Soviet Union-China: The Great Power Triangle*, Washington, DC: US Government Printing Office.

Howlett, Michael P. and M. Ramesh (1995) *Studying Public Policy: Policy Cycles and Policy Sub-systems*, Oxford: Oxford University Press: pp. 11–12.

Hudson, Valerie, 'Foreign Policy Analysis: Actor-Specific Theory and the Ground of International Relations', *Foreign Policy Analysis*, Vol. 1. No. 1, 2005, p. 1.

Hunt, Michael H. (1989) *Ideology and US Foreign Policy*, New Haven, CT: Yale University Press.

Huntington, Samuel P., Chan Heng Chee, Robert Bartley and Shijuro Ogata (1993) *Democracy and Capitalism: Asian and American Perspectives*, Singapore: ISEAS Press.

Hu Zhangming (2015) *Wisdom of Zhou Enlai: Why the Famous Became Famous* [大智周恩来: 伟人何以成为伟人], Beijing: Guangming Daily Press.

Hyer, Eric (2015) *The Pragmatic Dragon: China's Grand Strategy and Boundary Settlements*, Vancouver: UBC Press.

Immerman, Richard H. (2010) *Empire for Liberty: A History of American Imperialism from Benjamin Franklin to Paul Wolfowitz*, Princeton, NJ: Princeton University Press: p. 209.

ISEAS (2006) *Roundtable on Malaysia-Singapore Relations: Mending Fences and Making Good Neighbours*, Singapore: ISEAS Press.

Issacson, Walter (2005) *Kissinger: A Biography*, New York: Simon & Schuster.

Iyob, Ruth, 'The Eritrean Experiment: A Cautious Pragmatism?', *The Journal of Modern African Studies*, Vol. 35, No. 4, 1997, p. 667.

Jacques, Martin (2012) *When China Rules the World*, New York: Penguin.

Jain, Rajendra K., 'From Idealism to Pragmatism: India and Asian Regional Integration', *Japanese Journal of Political Science*, Vol. 12, No. 2, August 2011, pp. 227–228.

Jann, Werner and Kai Wegrich. 'Theories of the Policy Cycle', in Frank Fischer, Gerald J. Miller and Mara S. Sidney (Eds.) (2007), *Handbook of Public Policy Analysis*, Boca Raton, FL: CRC Press: p. 57.

Jayakumar, Shashi (2016) *State, Society and National Security: Challenges and Opportunities in the 21st Century*, Singapore: World Scientific.

Jayakumar, Shashi and Tommy Koh (2009) *Pedra Branca: The Road to the World Court*, Singapore: NUS Press.

Jayakumar, Shashi and Rahul Sagar (2015) *The Big Ideas of Lee Kuan Yew*, Singapore: Straits Times Press.

Jayakumar, Shunmugam (2015) *Be at the Table or Be on the Menu: A Singapore Memoir*, Singapore: Straits Times Press.

Jervis, Robert (1997) *Systems Effects: Complexity in Political and Social Life*, Princeton, NJ: Princeton University Press.

Ji You, 'Taiwan in the Political Calculations of the Chinese Leadership', *The China Journal*, Vol. 36, 1996, pp. 119–125.

Jia Qingguo and Yan Jun (Eds.) (2015) *New Type of Great Power Relations: Opportunities and Challenges* [新型大国关系: 机遇与挑战], Beijing: Peking University Press.

Jiang Zongqiang et al. (Trans.) (2012) *Does the 21st Century Belong to China? The Munk Debate on China* [环球时报, 争辩中国: 环球时报国际论坛十周年精品], Beijing: China Citic Press.

Jin Canrong (2011) *Big Power's Responsibility: China's Perspective*, Beijing: China Renmin University Press.

Jin Liqun and Justin Yifu Lin (Eds.) (2015) *One Belt One Road Leading China: National Strategic Design and Implementation* ["一带一路"引领中国: 国家顶层战略设计与行动布局], Beijing: China Historical Press.

Johnson, Neil (2007) *Two's Company, Three Is Complexity – A Simple Guide to the Science of All Sciences*, New York and London: One World Publications.

Jung Dietrich and Wolfango Piccoli, 'The Turkish-Israeli Alignment: Paranoia or Pragmatism?', *Security Dialogue*, Vol. 31, No. 1, 2000, pp. 91–104.

Kaag, John and Sarah Kreps, 'Pragmatism's Contributions to International Relations', *Cambridge Review of International Affairs*, Vol. 25, No. 2, June 2012, pp. 191–208.

Kamarck, Elaine C. (2016) *Why Presidents Fail and How They Can Succeed Again*, Washington, DC: Brookings Institution Press.

Kan, Shirley A. et al. (2002) 'China-US Aircraft Collision Incident of April 2001: Assessments and Policy Implications', Washington, DC: Congressional Report Services.

Kaplan, Robert D. (2017) *Earning the Rockies: How Geography Shapes America's Role in the World*, New York: Random House.

Kausikan, Bilahari (2017) *Dealing with an Ambiguous World*, Singapore: World Scientific.

Kausikan, Bilahari (2017) *Singapore Is Not an Island: Views on Singapore Foreign Policy*, Singapore: Straits Times Press.

Kesavapany, K. and Rahul Sen (2007) *Negotiating the Korea-Singapore FTA: A Case Study*, Singapore: ISEAS Press.

Khatib, Lina, 'Qatar's Foreign Policy: The Limits of Pragmatism', *International Affairs*, Vol. 89, No. 2, 2013, p. 420.

Khol, Radek, 'Czech Republic: Prague's Pragmatism', *Contemporary Security Policy*, Vol. 26, No. 3, December 2005, pp. 470–485.

Kirby, William C. et al. (2006) *The Normalization of US-China Relations: An International History*, Cambridge, MA: Harvard University Press.

Kissinger, Henry (1977) *American Foreign Policy*, New York: W. W. Norton & Company, pp. 24–25.

Klingler-Vidra, Robyn (2012) *The Pragmatic 'Little Red Dot': Singapore's US Hedge Against China*, London: LSE IDEAS.

Koh, Tommy (2013) *The Tommy Koh Reader: Favourite Essays and Lectures*, Singapore: World Scientific.

Koh, Tommy, Thong Bee, Kristin Paulson, Jose L. Tongzon and Vikram Khanna (2003) *US-Singapore FTA: Implications and Prospects*, Singapore: ISEAS Press.

Koh, Tommy and Li Lin Chang (2004) *The United States-Singapore Free Trade Agreement: Highlights and Insights*, Singapore: World Scientific.

Koh, Tommy and Li Lin Chang with Joanna Koh (2015) *50 Years of Singapore and the United Nations*, Singapore: World Scientific.

Koh, Tommy and Chang Li Lin (2005) *The Little Red Dot: Reflections by Singapore's Diplomats*, Singapore: World Scientific.

Koh, Tommy and Chang Li Lin (2009) *The Little Red Dot: Reflections by Singapore's Diplomats: Vol. II*, Singapore: World Scientific.

Koh, Tommy and Chang Li Lin (2015) *The Little Red Dot: Reflections of Foreign Ambassadors on Singapore*, Singapore: World Scientific.

Koh, Tommy, Sharon Li-lian Seah and Li Lin Chang (2017) *50 Years of ASEAN and Singapore*, Singapore: World Scientific.

Kwa Chong Guan (2006) *S. Rajaratnam on Singapore: From Ideas to Reality*, Singapore: World Scientific.

Kwa Chong Guan, Derek Thiam Soon Heng and Tai Yong Tan (2009) *Singapore, a 700-Year History: From Early Emporium to World City*, Singapore: National Archives of Singapore.

Lai Ah Eng (2008) *Religious Diversity in Singapore*, Singapore: ISEAS Press.

Lam Peng Er and Kevin Y. L. Tan (1999) *Lee's Lieutenants: Singapore's Old Guard*, New South Wales: Allen & Unwin.

Lampton, David M. (2014) *Following the Leader: Ruling China from Deng Xiaoping to Xi Jinping*, Berkeley, CA: California University Press.

Lasswell, Harold D. (1956) *The Decision Process: The Seven Categories of Functional Analysis*, College Park, MD: University of Maryland Press.

Latif, Asad-ul Iqbal (2007) *Between Rising Powers: China, Singapore and India*, Singapore: ISEAS Press.

Latif, Asad-ul Iqbal (2008) *Three Sides in Search of a Triangle: Singapore-America-India*, Singapore: ISEAS Press.

Latif, Asad-ul Iqbal and Lee Huay Leng (2015) *George Yeo: On Bonsai, Banyan and the Tao*, Singapore: World Scientific.

Layne, Christopher (2006) *The Peace of Illusions: American Grand Strategy from 1940 to the Present*, Ithaca, NY: Cornell University Press.

Lee, Charlotte P. (2015) *Training the Party*, Cambridge: Cambridge University Press.

Lee Hsien Loong. National Day Rally Speech, PMO, 14 August 2011. Accessed from: www.pmo.gov.sg/Newsroom/prime-minister-lee-hsien-loongs-national-day-rally-2011-speech-english. Accessed on 4 May 2019.

Lee Khoon Choy (1993) *Diplomacy of a Tiny State*, Singapore: World Scientific.

Lee Kuan Yew (1961) *Battle for Merger: 1961–1962*, Singapore: Straits Times Press.

Lee Kuan Yew. Speech to Nixon Center for Peace and Freedom, Washington, DC, 11 November 1996.

Lee Kuan Yew (1998) *The Singapore Story: Memoirs of Lee Kuan Yew*, Singapore: Prentice Hall.

Lee Kuan Yew (2000) *From Third World to First: The Singapore Story 1965–2000*, Singapore: Marshall Cavendish.

Lee Kuan Yew (2005) *Keeping My Mandarin Alive: Lee Kuan Yew's Language Learning Experience*, Singapore: World Scientific.

Lee Kuan Yew (2011) *My Lifelong Challenge: Singapore's Bilingual Journey*, Singapore: Straits Times Press.

Lee Kuan Yew (2013) *One Man's View of the World*, Singapore: Straits Times Press.

Lee Kuan Yew (2015) *The Wit and Wisdom of Lee Kuan Yew: 1923–2015*, Singapore: EDM.

Lee Kuan Yew and Janice Tay (2016) *Governance, Management and Life: A Collection of Quotes from Lee Kuan Yew*, Singapore: Straits Times Press.

Lee Poh Oon (2003) *The Water Issue Between Singapore and Malaysia: No Solution in Sight?* Singapore: ISEAS Press.

Lee Siew Cheng Edwin (2008) *Singapore: The Unexpected Nation*, Singapore: ISEAS Press.

Leifer, Michael (2000) *Singapore's Foreign Policy: Coping with Vulnerability*, Oxon: Routledge.

Levine, Steven I., 'China Policy During Carter's Year One', *Asian Survey*, Vol. 18, No. 5, 1978, pp. 437–447.

Lieberthal, Kenneth and David M. Lampton (Eds.) (1992) *Bureaucracy, Politics, and Decision Making in Post-Mao China*, Washington DC: Brookings Institution Press: pp. 357–401.

Lim, C. L. and Margaret Liang (2011) *Economic Diplomacy: Essays and Reflections by Singapore's Negotiators*, Singapore: World Scientific.

Lim Tai Wei (2017) *The Merlion and Mt. Fuji: 50 Years of Singapore-Japan Relations*, Singapore: World Scientific.

Liow Chinyong, Joseph and Ralf Emmers (2006) *Order and Security in Southeast Asia: Essays in Memory of Michael Leifer*, Oxon: Routledge.

Li Ruihuan (2010) *Practical and Truth-Seeking* [务实求理], Beijing: Renmin University Press.

Little, Richard. 'Preface', in Harry Bauer and Elisebetta Brighi (Eds.) (2009), *Pragmatism in International Relations*, Oxon: Routledge: pp. XII–XIII.

Liu Gretchen (2005) *The Singapore Foreign Service: The First 40 Years*, Singapore: EDM.

Liu Guoli (1994) *States and Markets: Comparing Japan and Russia*, Boulder, CO: Westview Press: pp. 103–104.

Liu Mingfu (2010) *The China Dream* [中国梦], Shanghai: China Friendship Publishing.

Lu Ning (2018) *The Dynamics of Foreign-Policy Decision Making in China*, London: Routledge.

Lu Yuan Li (2006) *Why Singapore Can Do It*, Jiangxi: Jiangxi Publishing House. Translated from: 吕元礼, 新加坡为什么能? (江西: 江西出版社), 2006.

Lu Yuan Li (2010) *Merlion Wisdom*, Beijing: Economy and Management Publishing House. Translated from: 吕元礼, 鱼尾狮智慧: 新加坡政治与治理, (北京: 经济管理出版社), 2010.

Lu Yuan Li (2011) *Why Singapore Is Able to Fix Corruption?* Guangzhou: Guangdong People's Publishing House. Translated from: 吕元礼, 新加坡治贪为什么能? (广州: 广东人民出版社), 2011.

Lu Yuan Li, Liu Xin, Liu Yu Hong and Zeng Yuan Li (2015) *How Singapore Effectively Govern? Ask Lee Kuan Yew*, Tianjin: Tianjin People's Publishing House. Translated from: 吕园礼, 刘歆, 刘宇红, 曾园俐, 新加坡如何有效治理: 问政李光耀, (天津: 天津出版社), 2015.

Luo Jianbo (Ed.) (2016) *Research into Big Power Diplomacy with Chinese Characteristics* [中国特色大国外交研究], Beijing: Chinese Social Sciences Press.

Luttwak, Edward N. (2012) *The Rise of China vs The Logic Strategy*, Cambridge, MA: Harvard University Press.

MacFarquhar, Roderick (Ed.) (1993) *The Politics of China, 1949–1989*, Cambridge: Cambridge University Press.

MacNeil, Neil and Richard A. Baker (2013) *The American Senate: An Insider's History*, New York: Oxford University Press.

Mahbubani, Kishore, "Treat China and Trump with Respect in 2017", *Straits Times*, 11 February 2017.

Maiden, Ben, 'Pragmatism the Strategy for Hong Kong and China', *International Financial Law*, Vol. 18, No. 5, May 1999, pp. 37–40.

Malachowski, Alan, 'Pragmatism: Overview', *SAGE Knowledge*, 15 January 2013.

Malone, David M. and Yuen Foong Khong (Eds.) (2003) *Unilateralism & US Foreign Policy: International Perspectives*, Boulder, CO: Lynne Rienner.

Mann, James (2000) *About Face: A History of America's Curious Relationship with China, from Nixon to Clinton*, New York: Vintage Books.

Mao Zedong, 'On Contradiction', *Chinese Studies in Philosophy*, Vol. 19, No. 2, 1987, pp. 20–82.

Mao Zedong (2007) *On Diplomacy*, Beijing: Foreign Languages Press.

Marinoff, Lou (2007) *The Middle Way: Finding Happiness in a World of Extremes*, New York: Sterling.

Marsh, David and Gerry Stoker (2010) *Theory and Methods in Political Science*, Basingstoke: Palgrave Macmillan: p. 291. J. S. Mill (1875) *A System of Logic Ratiocinative and Inductive: Vol. 2*, London: Longman.

Martel, William C. (2015) *Grand Strategy in the Theory and Practice: The Need for an Effective American Foreign Policy*, New York: Cambridge University Press.

Ma Shikun. 'Why President Carter Is Popular in China', *China US Focus*, 18 November 2015. Accessed from: www.chinausfocus.com/culture-history/why-president-carter-is-popular-in-china. Accessed on 31 December 2017.

Maya Guo (2015) *Trust in the Path: A New Model for a Rising Power*, Beijing: Foreign Languages Press.

Maya Guo (2015) *Trust in the Theory: China's Philosophy for a New International Order*, Beijing: Foreign Languages Press.

McDonald, Hamish, 'Mutual Benefits: A New Pragmatism Drives India's Burma Policy', *Far Eastern Economic Review*, 3 February 1994, p. 14.

McDougall, Walter A. (2016) *The Tragedy of US Foreign Policy: How America's Civil Religion Betrayed the National Interest*, New Haven, CT: Yale University Press.

Mead, Walter Russell (2002) *Special Providence: American Foreign Policy and How It Changed the World*, New York: Routledge.

Mearsheimer, John J., 'The Gathering Storm: China's Challenge to US Power in Asia', *The Chinese Journal of International Politics*, Vol. 3, No. 4, 2010, pp. 381–396.

Melakopides, Costas (1998) *Pragmatic Idealism Canadian Foreign Policy 1945–1995*, Montreal: McGill-Queen's University Press.

Menand, Louis (1997) *Pragmatism: A Reader*, New York: Vintage Books.

Menand, Louis (2001) *The Metaphysical Club: A Story of Ideas in America*, New York: Farrar Straus Giroux: p. 369.

Menashri, David, 'Iran's Regional Policy: Between Radicalism and Pragmatism', *Journal of International Affairs*, Vol. 60, No. 2, Spring 2007, pp. 153–166.

Menon, Ravi. Opening Address 'Markets and Government: Striking a Balance in Singapore', by Ravi Menon, Permanent Secretary, Ministry of Trade and Industry, at Singapore Economic Policy Forum at Grand Hyatt Singapore, 22 October 2010. Accessed from: http://ess.org.sg/Events/Files/2010/R_Menon_speech.pdf. Accessed on 31 March 2019.

Menon, Ravi, 'Economic Thinking and Practice in Singapore', *Ethos, Civil Service College*, No. 11, 14 August 2012. Accessed from: www.csc.gov.sg/articles/economic-thinking-and-practice-in-singapore. Accessed on 31 March 2019.

Mesa-Lago, Carmelo (1978) *Cuba in the 1970s: Pragmatism and Institutionalization*, New Mexico: University of New Mexico Press.

Miksic, John N. (2013) *Singapore and the Silk Road of the Sea 1300–1800*, Singapore: NUS Press.

Mill, J. S. (1875) *A System of Logic Ratiocinative and Inductive: Vol. 2*, London: Longman.

Mintz, Alex, 'How Do Leaders Make Decisions? A Poliheuristic Perspective', *Journal of Conflict Resolution*, Vol. 48, No. 1, 2004, pp. 3–13.

Mitchell, Melanie (2009) *Complexity: A Guided Tour*, Oxford: Oxford University Press.

Mohamad, Kadir (2015) *Malaysia Singapore: Fifty Years of Contentions 1965–2015*, Kuala Lumpur: The Other Press.

Monshipouri, Mahmood, 'Iran's Search for the New Pragmatism', *Middle East Policy*, Vol. 6, No. 2, October 1998, p. 108.

Morcol, Goktug (2012) *A Complexity Theory for Public Policy*, New York: Routledge.

Morris, Roger (1977) *Uncertain Greatness*, New York: Harper & Row.

Nathan, Andrew and Robert Ross (1997) *The Great Wall and the Empty Fortress*, New York: W. W. Norton & Company.

Nathan, James A. and James K. Oliver (1994) *Foreign Policy Making and the American Political System*, Baltimore, MD: Johns Hopkins University Press.

Nazario, Olga (1983) *Pragmatism in Brazilian Foreign Policy: The Geisel Years, 1974–79*, Ph.D. dissertation, Ann Arbor, MI: University of Michigan.

Neo Boon Siong and Geraldine Chen (2007) *Dynamic Governance: Embedding Culture, Capabilities and Change in Singapore*, Singapore: World Scientific.

The New Paper (2008) *Founding Fathers*, Singapore: SNP.

Ng, Irene (2010) *The Singapore Lion: A Biography of S. Rajaratnam*, Singapore: ISEAS Press.

Nixon, Richard M., 'Asia After Vietnam', *Foreign Affairs*, Vol. 46, October 1967.

Noorderhaven, Niels G., Jos Benders and Arjan B. Keizer, 'Comprehensiveness Versus Pragmatism: Consensus at the Japanese-Dutch Interface', *Journal of Management Studies*, Vol. 44, No. 8, December 2007, pp. 1349–1370.

Nye, Joseph S. (2004) *Soft Power: The Means to Success in World Politics*, New York: Public Affairs.

Oakeshott, Michael (1933) *Experience and Its Modes*, Cambridge: Cambridge University Press.

Oei, Anthony (2005) *Days of Thunder: How Lee Kuan Yew Blazed the Freedom Trail*, 2nd edn., Singapore: Marshall Cavendish.

Ooi Kee Beng (2010) *In Lieu of Ideology: An Intellectual Biography of Goh Keng Swee*, Singapore: ISEAS Press.

Pang, Eul-Soo (2011) *The United States-Singapore Free Trade Agreement: An American Perspective on Power, Trade and Security in the Asia-Pacific*, Singapore: ISEAS Press.

Peh, Shing Huei (2019) *Tall Order: The Goh Chok Tong Story*, Singapore: World Scientific Publishing Company Pte. Limited.

Pillar, Paul R. (2016) *Why America Misunderstands the World: National Experience and Roots of Misperception*, New York: Columbia University Press.

Pilon, Maxime and Daniele Weiler (2011) *The French in Singapore: An Illustrated History (1819-Today)*, Singapore: EDM.

Plate, Tom (2010) *Conversations with Lee Kuan Yew: How to Build a Nation*, Singapore: Marshall Cavendish.

Popescu, Ionut C. (2017) *Emergent Strategy and Grand Strategy: How American Presidents Succeed in Foreign Policy*, Baltimore, MD: Johns Hopkins University Press.

Popescu, Ionut C., 'Grand Strategy vs. Emergent Strategy in the Conduct of Foreign Policy', *Journal of Strategic Studies*, Vol. 41, No. 3, 2018.

Preston, Andrew (2012) *Sword of the Spirit, Shield of Faith: Religion in American War and Diplomacy*, New York: Anchor Books.

Priess, David (2016) *The President's Book of Secrets: The Untold Story of Intelligence Briefings to America's Presidents*, New York: Public Affairs.

Public Service Division (2015) *Heart of Public Service: Our People, Our Institutions*, Singapore: Public Service Division.

Pye, Lucian W. (1968) *The Spirit of Chinese Politics: A Psychocultural Study of the Authority Crisis in Political Development*, Cambridge, MA: Massachusetts Institute of Technology Press.

Pye, Lucian W., 'On Chinese Pragmatism in the 1980s', *The China Quarterly*, No. 106, June 1986, pp. 207–234.

Qin Yaqing (2011) *Great Power Relations and China's Diplomacy* [大国关系与中国外交], Beijing: World Affairs Press.

Qiu Huafei (2013) *Contemporary Chinese Foreign Affairs and International Relations*, Beijing: Current Affairs Press.

Quah, Jon S. T. (2010) *Public Administration Singapore Style*, Singapore: Talisman.

Rahim, Lily Zubaidah (2009) *Singapore in the Malay World: Building and Breaching Regional Bridges*, Oxon: Routledge.

Rajan, M. S., 'Pragmatism in India's Foreign Policy', *South Asian Survey*, Vol. 1, No. 1, 1994, pp. 87–89.

Rajan, Ramkishen S., Rahul Sen and Reza Yamora (2001) *Singapore and Free Trade Agreements: Economic Relations with Japan and United States*, Singapore: ISEAS Press.

Ralston, Shane J., 'Pragmatism in International Relations Theory and Research', *Eidos*, Vol. 14, 2011, pp. 72–105.

Ralston, Shane J. (2013) *Philosophical Pragmatism and International Relations: Essays for a Bold New World*, Plymouth: Lexington Books.

Ramazani, R. K., 'Ideology and Pragmatism in Iran's Foreign Policy', *Middle East Journal*, Vol. 58, No. 4, Autumn 2004, pp. 549–550.

Reagan, Ronald. 'Remarks to Chinese Community Leaders in Beijing, China', 27 April 1984. Accessed from: www.presidency.ucsb.edu/ws/index.php?pid=39831. Accessed on 31 December 2017.

Rhodes, Mary Lee, Joanne Murphy, Jenny Muir and John A. Murray (2011) *Public Management and Complexity Theory: Richer Decision-making in Public Service*, New York: Routledge.

Richard Rosecrance and Gu Guoliang (Eds.) (2009) *Power and Restraint: A Shared Vision for the US-China Relationship*, New York: Public Affairs.

Ripsman, Norrin M., Jeffrey W. Taliaferro and Steven E. Lobell (2016) *Neoclassical Realist Theory of International Politics*, New York: Oxford University Press: p. 163.

Robert B. Talisse and Scott F. Aikin (2011) *The Pragmatism Reader: From Peirce Through the Present*, Princeton, NJ: Princeton University Press.

Robinson, Linda, 'Communism or Pragmatism: Fidel Castro', *US News & World Report*, Vol. 115, No. 25, 1994.

Robinson, Thomas W., 'Chou En-lai's Political Style: Comparisons with Mao Tse-Tung and Lin Piao', *Asian Survey*, Vol. 10, No. 12, December 1970, pp. 1101–1116.

Rose, Gideon, 'Neoclassical Realism and Theories of Foreign Policy', *World Politics*, Vol. 51, No. 1, 1998, pp. 144–172.

Rozman, Gilbert (2010) *Chinese Strategic Thought Towards Asia*, New York: Palgrave Macmillan.

Rynhold, Jonathan, 'China's Cautious New Pragmatism in the Middle East', *Survival: Global Politics and* Strategy, Vol. 38, No. 3, Autumn 1996, pp. 102–116.

Salvado, Francisco Romero, ' "Fatal Neutrality": Pragmatism or Capitulation? Spain's Foreign Policy During the Great War', *European History Quarterly*, Vol. 3, No. 3, 2003, pp. 291–315.

Saw Swee-Hock and K. Kesavapany (2006) *Singapore-Malaysia Relations Under Abdullah Badawi*, Singapore: ISEAS Press.

Saw Swee-Hock and John Wong (2014) *Advancing Singapore-China Economic Relations*, Singapore: ISEAS Press.

Scheffler, Israel (1986) *Four Pragmatists: A Critical Introduction to Perice, James, Mead and Dewey*, London: Routledge and Kegan Paul.

Schein, Edgar (1996) *Strategic Pragmatism: The Culture of Singapore's Economic Development Board*, Cambridge, MA: Massachusetts Institute of Technology Press.

Schell, Orville and John Delury (2014) *Wealth and Power: China's Long March to the Twenty-First Century*, New York: Random House Trade Paperbacks.

Schmiegelow, Michele and Henrick Schmiegelow (1989) *Strategic Pragmatism: Japanese Lessons in the Use of Economic Theory*, New York: Praeger: p. 160.

Schreer, Benjamin, 'A New "Pragmatism": Germany's NATO Policy', *International Journal*, Vol. 64, No. 2, *NATO at 60*, Spring 2009, p. 392.

Sen, Rahul (2008) *Trade Policy and the Role of Regional and Bilateral FTAs: The Case of New Zealand and Singapore*, Singapore: ISEAS Press.

Senge, Peter M., Art Kleiner, Charlotte Roberts, Richard B. Ross and Bryan J. Smith (1994) *The Fifth Discipline Fieldbook: Strategies and Tools for Building a Learning Organization*, New York: Random House.

Shambaugh, David (2013) *China Goes Global: The Partial Power*, New York: Oxford University Press.

Shao Kuo-Kang (1996) *Zhou Enlai and the Foundations of Chinese Foreign Policy*, New York: St Martin's Press.

Shiraishi, Takashi (2009) *Across the Causeway: A Multi-Dimensional Study of Malaysia-Singapore Relations*, Singapore: ISEAS Press.

Shlapentokh, Dmitry, 'Putin's Moscow Approach to Iran: Between Pragmatism and Fear', *Journal of Balkan and Near Eastern Studies*, Vol. 13, No. 2, June 2011, pp. 190, 199–200, 203.

Short, Philip (2016) *Mao: The Man Who Made China*, London: Bloomsbury Publishing.

Shusterman, Richard (2004) *The Range of Pragmatism and the Limits of Philosophy*, Oxon: Blackwell.

Sil, Rudra and Peter J. Katzenstein (2010) *Beyond Paradigms: Analytic Eclecticism in the Study of World Politics*, London: Palgrave Macmillan.

Sim, Susan (2016) *E. W. Barker: The People's Minister*, Singapore: Straits Times Press.

Simon, Herbert and James March (1976) *Administrative Behavior Organization*, New York: Free Press.

Singh, Bilveer (1999) *The Vulnerability of Small States Revisited: A Study of Singapore's Post-Cold War Foreign Policy*, Yogyakarta: Gadjah Mada University Press.

Singh, Bilveer (2007) *Politics and Governance in Singapore: An Introduction*, Singapore: McGraw-Hill.

Singh Sandhu, Kernial and Paul Wheatley (1989) *Management of Success: The Moulding of Modern Singapore*, Singapore: ISEAS Press.

Slim, Bouchaib (2007) *Singapore Through Arab Eyes*, Singapore: ISEAS Press.

Smith, Tony (2017) *Why Wilson Matters: The Origins of American Liberal Internationalism and Its Crisis Today*, Princeton, NJ: Princeton University Press.

Somjee, H. and Geeta Somjee (1995) *Development Success in Asia Pacific: An Exercise in Normative-Pragmatic Balance*, New York: St Martin's Press.

Song Haixiao (2015) *Pattern of Decision-Making of Chinese Foreign Policy* [中国外交策模式], Guangzhou: Guangdong University of Foreign Studies.

Song Qiang et al. (1996) *China Can Say No* [中国可以说不: 冷战后时代的政治与情感抉择], Beijing: China Federation of Literary and Arts Circle Press.

Song Xiaojun et al. (2009) *Unhappy China: The Great Time, Grand Vision and Our Challenges* [中国不高兴: 大时代, 大目标及我们的内忧外患], Nanjing: Jiangsu People's Press.

Special Issue on Pragmatism, *Millennium Journal of International Studies*, Vol. 31, No. 3, 2002. Accessed from: https://journals.sagepub.com/toc/mila/31/3.

State Department. 'The August 17 1982 US-China Communique on Arms Sales to Taiwan'. Accessed from: https://history.state.gov/milestones/1981-1988/china-communique. Accessed on 31 December 2017.

Stephens, Philip, 'Cameron's Coalition Has Opted for Pragmatism', *Financial Times*, 13 May 2010.

Stoessinger, John G. (1985) *Crusaders and Pragmatists: Movers of Modern American Foreign Policy*, New York: W. W. Norton & Company.

Storey, Ian, Ralf Emmers and Daljit Singh (2011) *The Five Power Defence Arrangements at Forty*, Singapore: ISEAS Press.

The Straits Times (2015) *Lee's Legacy*, Singapore: Straits Times Press.

The Straits Times (2015) *Lee Kuan Yew: A Tribute*, Singapore: Straits Times Press.

The Straits Times (2016) *Vintage Lee: Landmark Speeches Since 1955*, Singapore: Straits Times Press.

Suettinger, Robert L. (2003) *Beyond Tiananmen: The Politics of U.S.-China Relations 1989–2000*, Washington, DC: Brookings Institution Press: p. 420.

Sun Zhi et al. (2014) *China-US Relations: Managing Differences and Cooperation in Development* [Zhong-Mei Waijiao: Guankong Fenqi yu Hezuo Fazhan], Beijing: Current Affairs Press.

Sutter, Robert (1983) *The China Quandary: Domestic Determinants of US China Policy, 1972–1982*, Boulder, CO: Westview Press.

Sutter, Robert, 'The Taiwan Problem in the Second George W. Bush Administration – US Officials' Views and Their Implications for US Policy', *Journal of Contemporary China*, Vol. 15, No. 48, 2006.

Sutter, Robert G. (2013) *Foreign Relations of the PRC: The Legacies and Constraints of China's International Politics Since 1949*, Lanham, MD: Rowman & Littlefield.

Swaine, Michael D. and Ashley J. Tellis (2000) *Interpreting China's Grand Strategy: Past, Present and Future*, Santa Monica, CA: RAND Corp.

Takeyh, Ray and Nikloas K. Gvosdev, 'Pragmatism in the Midst of Iranian Turmoil', *The Washington Quarterly*, Vol. 27, No. 4, Autumn 2004, pp. 35–39.

Taleb Fares, Seme, 'The Oil Pragmatism: The Brazil-Iraq Relations', *Revista Brasileira de Política Internacional*, Vol. 50, No. 2, 2007, pp. 129–145.

Talisse, Robert B. and Scott F. Aikin (2008) *Pragmatism: A Guide for the Perplexed*, New York: Continuum: p. 25.

Tan, Kenneth Paul, 'The Ideology of Pragmatism: Neo-Liberal Globalisation and Political Authoritarianism in Singapore', *Journal of Contemporary Asia*, Vol. 42, No. 1, February 2012, pp. 67–92.

Tan, Kenneth Paul (2017) *Governing Global-city Singapore: Legacies and Futures After Lee Kuan Yew*, Oxon: Routledge.

Tan, Kenneth Paul (2018) *Singapore: Identity, Brand, Power*, Cambridge: Cambridge University Press.

Tan Siok Sun (2007) *Goh Keng Swee: A Portrait*, Singapore: EDM.

Tan Sor-Hoon, 'China's Pragmatist Experiment in Democracy: Hu Shih's Pragmatism and Dewey's Influence in China', *Metaphilosophy*, Vol. 35, No. ½, January 2004, pp. 44–64.

Tao Wenzhao (2015) *A Brief History of China-US Relations: 1784–2013*, Beijing: Foreign Languages Press.

Tarling, Nicholas (2012) *Studying Singapore's Past: C. M. Turnbull and the History of Modern Singapore*, Singapore: NUS Press.

Tay, Simon S. C. (2006) *A Mandarin and the Making of Public Policy*, Singapore: NUS Press.

Tian Yongxiang (2012) *International Relations of the Communist Party of China*, Beijing: China Intercontinental Press.

Toh, Elgin, 'Singapore Must Work Hard at Staying Relevant: Chan Chun Sing', *Straits Times*, 31 October 2017.

Tong Chee Kiong. 'Materialism, Pragmatism and the Pursuit of Happiness in Singapore', in Kenji Kosaka and Masahiro Ogino (Eds.) (2008), *A Quest for Alternative Sociology*, Melbourne: Trans Pacific Press.

Tsygankov, Andrei P., 'Two Faces of Putin's Great Power Pragmatism', *The Soviet and Post-Soviet Review*, Vol. 34, No. 1, 2007, pp. 104, 110.

Tu Wei Ming (2013) *Singapore's Challenge: Neo-Confucian Ethics and Entrepreneurial Spirit*, Beijing: Sanlian Book. Translated from: 杜维明, 新加坡的挑战: 新儒家理论与企业精神, (北京: 生活读书新知三联书店), 2013.

Tung, William L. (2012) *The Political Institutions of Modern China*, Berlin: Springer Science & Business Media.

Turnbull, Constance M. (2009) *A History of Modern Singapore: 1819–2005*, Singapore: NUS Press.

Vandenborre, Alain (2005) *The Little Door to the New World: China-Singapore-India*, Singapore: SNP.

Van Riper, Paul P. 'The Politics-Administration Dichotomy', in Jack Rabin and James Bowman (Eds.) (1984), *Politics and Administration: Woodrow Wilson and American Public Administration*, New York: Marcel Dekker Inc. pp. 203–217.

Van Vranke Hickey, Dennis (2007) *Foreign Policy Making in Taiwan: From Principle to Pragmatism*, Oxon: Routledge.

Various authors (2015) *Up Close with Lee Kuan Yew: Insights from Colleagues and Friends*, Singapore: Marshall Cavendish.

Vasil, Raj (2000) *Governing Singapore: A History of National Development and Democracy*, Singapore: ISEAS Press.

Vassiliev, Alexei (1993) *Russian Policy in the Middle East: From Messianism to Pragmatism*, Reading: Ithaca Press.

Vihma, Antto, 'India and the Global Climate Governance: Between Principles and Pragmatism', *The Journal of Environment & Development*, Vol. 20, No. 1, January 2011, pp. 69–94.

Walt, Stephen M. (2006) *Taming American Power: The Global Response to US Primacy*, New York: W. W. Norton & Company.

Walters, Vernon A. (1978) *Silent Missions*, New York: Doubleday & Co.

Wang, Jessica Ching-Sze (2012) *John Dewey in China: To Teach and to Learn*, New York: State University of New York Press.

Wang Fan (2016) *Big-Power Diplomacy* [大国外交], Beijing: Beijing United Publishing.

Wang Jian et al. (2003) *New Warring States Period* [新战国时代], Beijing: Xinhua Press.

Wang Jisi (2015) *Great Power Relations: US-China Relations Converges or Diverges?* [大国关系: 中美分道扬镳, 还是殊途同归], Beijing: China Citic Press.

Wang Yizhou (2011) *Creative Involvement: A New Direction in China's Diplomacy* [创造性介入: 中国外交新取向], Beijing: Beijing University Press.

Wang Zhongchun and Cai Jingsong (2016) *China vs USA on the Grand Chessboard* [中美对弈大棋局], Beijing: Ocean Press.

Weil, Henry, 'The Shanghai Communiqué Five Years Later', *Change: The Magazine of Higher Learning*, Vol. 9, No. 5, 1977, pp. 14–16.

Welsh, Bridget, James Chin, Arun Mahizhnan and Tan Tarn How (2009) *Impressions of the Goh Chok Tong Years in Singapore*, Singapore: NUS Press.

Wendt, Alexander, 'Anarchy Is What States Make of It: The Social Construction of Power Politics', *International Organization*, Vol. 46, No. 2, 1992.

West, Cornel (1989) *The American Evasion of Philosophy*, Madison, WI: University of Wisconsin Press: p. 3.

Westbrook, Robert (2005) *Democratic Hope*, Ithaca, NY: Cornell University Press.

Wilairat, Kawin (1975) *Singapore's Foreign Policy*, Singapore: ISEAS Press.

Wilson, Peter, 'The Myth of the "First Great Debate"', *Review of International Studies*, Vol. 24, No. 5, 1998, pp. 1–16.

Wittkopf, Eugene R. and James M. McCormick (Eds.) (2008) *The Domestic Sources of American Foreign Policy: Insights and Evidence*, Lanham, MD: Rowman & Littlefield.

Wu Jianming (2006) *Foreign Policy and International Relations: Views and Analysis from Wu Jianming* [外交与国际关系: 吴建民的看法与思考], Beijing: Renmin University Press.

Xi Jinping (2014) *The Governance of China*, Beijing: Foreign Languages Press.

Xiao Shimei (2013) *Wisdom of Mao Zedong* [毛泽东智慧], Beijing: People's Press.

Xie Yixian et al. (Eds.) (2009) *Contemporary Chinese Diplomatic History: 1949–2009* [中国当代外交史], Beijing: China Youth Publishing House.

Xiong Zhiyong et al. (2015) *Lectures on China-US Relations* [中美关系讲义], Beijing: World Knowledge Press.

Xu Guoqi (2014) *Chinese and Americans: A Shared History*, Cambridge, MA: Harvard University Press.

Yahya, Yasmine, 'Lim Hng Kiang: Longest-serving MTI Minister Who Prefers Talking Trade to Getting Personal', *Straits Times*, 27 April 2018.

Yan Sheng Yi (2009) *Contemporary Foreign Affairs of China* [外交理论与实务], Shanghai: Fudan University Press.

Yan Xuetong, 'The Rise of China and Its Power Status', *The Chinese Journal of International Politics*, Vol. 1, No. 1, 2006, pp. 5–33.

Yan Xuetong (2013) *Ancient Chinese Thought, Modern Chinese Power*, Princeton, NJ: Princeton University Press.

Yang Chen-Ning, Ying-Shih Yu, Gungwu Wang and others (2017) *Lee Kuan Yew: Through the Eyes of Chinese Scholars*, Singapore: World Scientific.

Yang Jiemian, 'China's "New Diplomacy" Under the Xi Jinping Administration', *China Quarterly of International Strategic Studies*, Vol. 1, No. 1, 2015, pp. 1–17.

Yang Jiemian (2015) *Contemporary Thought in Chinese Foreign Policy: Innovation in Strategy and Practice* [新时期中国外交思想、战略和实践的探索创新], Shanghai: Shanghai People's Publishing House.

Yang Ye et al. (Eds.) (2008) *Foreign Policy Theory and Practice* [外交理论与实务], Beijing: Foreign Language Teaching and Research Press.

Yaqub, Salim, 'John Foster Dulles: Piety, Pragmatism and Power in US Foreign Policy (Review)', *Journal of Cold War Studies*, Vol. 4, No. 3, Summer 2002, pp. 123–125.

Yeo Lay Hwee, Peggy Kek, Gillian Koh and Chang Li Lin (2018) *Tommy Koh: Serving Singapore and the World*, Singapore: World Scientific.

Yeo Lay Hwee and Bernard Turner (2015) *50 Years of Singapore-Europe Relations: Celebrating Singapore's Connections with Europe*, Singapore: World Scientific.

Yip Wai Yee, 'Mediacorp Apologises for Remarks on Najib in TV Show', *Straits Times*, 6 April 2017.

Youde, Jeremy, 'Why Look East? Zimbabwean Foreign Policy and China', *Africa Today*, Vol. 53, No. 3, Spring 2007, pp. 3–19.

Yu Dingbang et al. (2015) *Diplomatic History of China and Southeast Asia: Qing Dynasty* [近代中国与东南亚关系史], Guangzhou: World Book Publishing Group.

Yu Huaiyan (2015) *Unfolding America: Pragmatism and Three Hundred Years of America* [深层美国: 实用主义与美国的300年], Beijing: Youyi Press [北京: 中国友谊出版公司].

Yu Wanli. 'Breaking the Cycle? Sino-US Relations under George W. Bush Administration', in (2009), *China's Shift: Global Strategy of the Rising Power*, Tokyo, Japan: National Institute for Defense Studies.

Yusuf Shahid and Kaoru Nabeshima (2011) *Some Small Countries Do It Better: Rapid Growth and Its Causes in Singapore, Finland and Ireland*, Washington, DC: World Bank.

Zangger, Andreas (2013) *The Swiss in Singapore*, Singapore: EDM.

Zhang Lili (2015) *A Brief History of Contemporary Chinese Diplomacy: 1949–2014* [当代中国外交简史], Shanghai: Shanghai People's Publishing House.

Zhang Qingmin (2010) *China's Diplomacy*, Beijing: China Intercontinental Press.

Zhang Qingmin (2014) *Contemporary China's Diplomacy*, Beijing: China Intercontinental Press.

Zhang Wei-Wei (1996) *Ideology and Economic Reform Under Deng Xiaoping, 1978–1993*, London: Routledge.

Zhang Zhibin (2011) *Dynamics of the Singapore Success Story: Insights by Ngiam Tong Dow*, Singapore: Cengage Learning.

Zhao Jinjun and Chen Zhirui (Eds.) (2013) *Participation and Interaction: The Theory and Practice of China's Diplomacy*, Hackensack, NJ: World Century.

Zhao Jinjun and Chen Zhirui (Eds.) (2014) *China and the International Society: Adaptation and Self-Consciousness*, Hackensack, NJ: World Century.

Zhao Qizheng (2009) *Dialogue Between Nations: Speeches by Zhao Qizheng*, Beijing: Foreign Languages Press.

Zhao Qizheng et al. (2010) *The China Model*, Beijing: New World Press.

Zhao Suisheng (2004) *Chinese Foreign Policy: Pragmatism and Strategic Behaviour*, New York: M. E. Sharpe.

Zheng Yongnian (2014) *Geopolitics: China's Rise Should Go Beyond Emotions and Ideology* [大格局: 中国崛起应该超越情感和意识形态], Beijing: Eastern Press.

Zheng Yongnian and Lye Liang Fook (2016) *Singapore-China Relations: 50 Years*, Singapore: World Scientific.

Zhu Rongji (2013) *Zhu Rongji on the Record: The Road to Reform 1991–1997*, Washington, DC: Brookings Institution Press.

Zhuang Fulin (Ed.) (2010) *Thought of Mao Zedong* [毛泽东思想概论], Beijing: Renmin University Press.

Interviews

The author wishes to thank all those who gave so generously of their time in contributing to this research.

China

Chen Zhirui, 4 July 2016
Chu Shulong, 18 August 2016
Cui Liru, 9 March 2017
Cui Tian Kai, 24 April 2017
Da Wei, 8 March 2017
Feng Yue, 25 December 2016
Jin Canrong, 25 December 2016
Li Ming Jiang, 16 February 2017
Justin Yifu Lin, 18 July 2016
Ma Zheng Gang, 2 March 2017
Niu Jun, 2 December 2016
Pan Wei, 25 July 2016
Qin Yaqing, 25 July 2016
David Shambaugh, 27 February 2017
Shi Yinhong, 29 June 2016
Su Hao, 1 July 2016
Sun Ge, 9 March 2017
Sun Yan, 7 March 2017
Sun Zhe, 25 April 2017
James Tang, 20 December 2016
Ezra Vogel, 17 May 2017
Wang Gungwu, 12 August 2016
Wang Jisi, 4 July 2016
Wang Yizhou, 20 July 2016
Wang Zhengyi, 24 July 2016

Victoria Wei, 20 July 2016
Wilson Wong, 2 August 2016
Xue Li, 19 August 2016
Yao Yun-Zhu, 30 June 2016
Ye Zhi Cheng, 7 March 2017
Yu Lei, 29 June 2016
Zhang Baijia, 24 July 2016
Zhang Qingmin, 7 March 2017
Zhang Tuosheng, 23 May 2017
Zhang Yunling, 8 March 2017
Zhao Tingyang, 20 August 2016
Zheng Yongnian, 3 February 2017
Zhu Cheng Hu, 10 March 2017

Singapore

Amitav Acharya, 13 February 2017
S. Dhanabalan, 17 January 2018
Cham Tao Soon, 3 April 2017
Chiang Chie Foo, 2 March 2017
Alan Chong, 15 December 2016
Han Fook Kwang, 5 April 2017
Bilahari Kausikan, 25 December 2016
Tommy Koh, 9 December 2016
Lim Siong Guan, 3 April 2017
Kishore Mahbubani, 1 March and 11 April 2017
Ravi Menon, 8 February 2017
Tan Chin Tiong, 10 February 2017
Kenneth Paul Tan, 27 December 2016
Wong Kan Seng, 13 February 2017
George Yeo, 1 February 2017
Zainal Abidin Rashid, 1 March 2017

United States

Richard Armitage, 2 August 2017
Richard Betts, 25 April 2017
Sarah Binder, 26 July 2017
David Brady, 5 June 2017
Hal Brands, 30 May 2017
Richard Bush, 22 May 2017
Fritjof Capra, 5 June 2017

James Clad, 2 August 2017
Steve Clemons, 24 November 2016
Eliot Cohen, 26 May 2017
John Donahue, 15 May 2017
Walter Douglas, 1 August 2017
Amitai Etzioni, 26 May 2017
Niall Ferguson, 18 July 2017
Carla Freeman, 27 July 2017
Chas Freeman, 1 June and 25 July 2017
Fung Archon, 15 May 2017
Nirmal Ghosh, 2 June 2017
Stephen Goldsmith, 15 May 2017
Michael Green, 27 July 2017
Marc Grossman, 10 July 2017
Richard Immerman, 11 June 2017
Robert Jervis, 14 April 2017
Elaine Kamarck, 26 July 2017
Thomas Keaney, 24 May 2017
Donald Kettl, 28 July 2017
Peter Kuznick, 28 July 2017
Ashok Kumar Mirpuri, 30 May 2017
David Lampton, 11 July 2017
Marc Landy, 15 May 2017
Frank Lavin 21 July 2017
Robert Lieber, 2 August 2017
James Loi, 26 May 2017
Thomas Mahnken, 2 August 2017
Michael Mandelbaum, 23 May 2017
James March, 19 July 2017
Louis Marinoff, 11 May 2017
Louis Menand, 15 May 2017
Steven Miller, 16 May 2017
Andrew Nathan, 1 May 2017
John Negroponte, 1 August 2017
Joseph S. Nye Jr., 9 May 2017
Michael O'Hanlon, 2 August 2017
Douglas Paal 24 July 2017
Tom Plate, 13 June 2017
Jeremy Rosner, 27 July 2017
Robert Ross, 9 May 2017
Stapleton Roy, 24 July 2017
Edgar Schein, 5 June 2017

Stephen Schlesinger, 11 May 2017
Steve Sestanovich, 1 August 2017
Nicholas Snyder, 26 May 2017
Jack Snyder, 11 May 2017
James Steinberg, 26 July 2017
Charles Stevenson, 22 May 2017
Joseph Stiglitz, 18 May 2017
Michael Swaine, 26 July 2017
Strobe Talbott, 21 July 2017
Stephen Walt, 16 May 2017

Questionnaires

Interview Questions For 'Varieties of Pragmatism in Foreign Policy'

Singapore

Definitions

1 How do you define Pragmatism?
2 In your opinion, is there a difference between the way practitioners and academics define Pragmatism?

Country Pragmatism

3 What do you think are the sources of inspiration for Pragmatism in Singapore? Historical context? Geographical size? Military power? Economic power? Diplomatic power? Political system? Stage of development? Socio-culture? Philosophy/ideology? Personalities?
4 Could you share examples of Pragmatism at play in Singapore foreign policy? (especially in Singapore–China, Singapore–US relations) With emphasis on the policy thinking, strategic communication to external and domestic audience, actual actions taken.
5 What is your take on US and Chinese Pragmatism? Is it different from Singapore's? How so? With emphasis on Historical context? Geographical size? Military power? Economic power? Diplomatic power? Political system? Stage of development? Socio-culture? Philosophy/ Ideology? Personalities?

Pragmatism in Action Incidents

6 Could you share examples of Pragmatism at play in Taiwan/East China Sea/South China Sea involving the US, China, Singapore and other

players? With emphasis on the policy thinking, strategic communication to external and domestic audience, actual actions taken from your perspective.

Academics Only

7 How could we operationalise Pragmatism into an academic model that can be measurable and use to ascertain if a particular action is pragmatic or not?
8 How would you distinguish Pragmatism from Realism, Liberalism and other IR ideologies?

Practitioners Only

9 How could we operationalise Pragmatism in practitioner world? Any examples to share? Is Pragmatism measurable?
10 Is it true that all practitioners are pragmatic? Is Pragmatism without principles, values?

China

Definitions

1 How do you define Pragmatism?
2 In your opinion, is there a difference between the way practitioners and academics define Pragmatism?

Country Pragmatism

3 What do you think are the sources of inspiration for Pragmatism in China? Historical context? Geographical size? Military power? Economic power? Diplomatic power? Political system? Stage of development? Socio-culture? Philosophy/ideology? Personalities?
4 Could you share examples of Pragmatism at play in Chinese foreign policy (especially in China–US, China–Singapore relations)? With emphasis on the policy thinking, strategic communication to external and domestic audience, actual actions taken.
5 What is your take on US and Singapore Pragmatism? Is it different from China's? How so? With emphasis on historical context? Geographical size? Military power? Economic power? Diplomatic power? Political system? Stage of development? Socio-culture? Philosophy/ideology? Personalities?

Pragmatism in Action Incidents

6   Could you share examples of Pragmatism at play in Taiwan/East China Sea/South China Sea involving the US, China, Singapore and other players? With emphasis on the policy thinking, strategic communication to external and domestic audience, actual actions taken from your perspective.

Academics Only

7   How could we operationalise Pragmatism into an academic model that can be measurable and use to ascertain if a particular action is pragmatic or not?
8   How would you distinguish Pragmatism from Realism, Liberalism and other IR ideologies?

Practitioners Only

9   How could we operationalise Pragmatism in practitioner world? Any examples to share? Is Pragmatism measurable?
10 Is it true that all practitioners are pragmatic? Is Pragmatism without principles, values?

US

Definitions

1   How do you define Pragmatism?
2   In your opinion, is there a difference between the way practitioners and academics define Pragmatism?

Country Pragmatism

3   What do you think are the sources of inspiration for Pragmatism in the US? Historical context? Geographical size? Military power? Economic power? Diplomatic power? Political system? Stage of development? Socio-culture? Philosophy/ideology? Personalities?
4   Could you share examples of Pragmatism at play in US foreign policy (especially in US–China, US–Singapore relations)? With emphasis on the policy thinking, strategic communication to external and domestic audience, actual actions taken.
5   What is your take on Chinese and Singapore Pragmatism? Is it different from that of the US? How so? With emphasis on historical context?

Geographical size? Military power? Economic power? Diplomatic power? Political system? Stage of development? Socio-culture? Philosophy/ideology? Personalities?

Pragmatism in Action Incidents

6 Could you share examples of Pragmatism at play in Taiwan/East China Sea/South China Sea involving the US, China, Singapore and other players? With emphasis on the policy thinking, strategic communication to external and domestic audience, actual actions taken from your perspective.

Academics Only

7 How could we operationalise Pragmatism into an academic model that can be measurable and use to ascertain if a particular action is pragmatic or not?
8 How would you distinguish Pragmatism from Realism, Liberalism and other IR ideologies?

Practitioners Only

9 How could we operationalise Pragmatism in practitioner world? Any examples to share? Is Pragmatism measurable?
10 Is it true that all practitioners are pragmatic? Is Pragmatism without principles, values?

Index

Note: Page numbers in bold indicate a table on the corresponding page.

5-step model (policy cycle) 23

Afghanistan 99
'Agendas and Instability'
  (Baumgartner and Jones) 23
agenda-setting 20; 'Agendas and
  Instability' on 23; ideological 51;
  international 26; national 24; and
  policy formulation 38, 60, 90;
  stage 51–54, 59, 96, 98, 104
agential factors of (pragmatic)
  production 18–20
Allison's Third Model of
  Governmental Politics 20
*American Diplomacy and the
  Pragmatic Tradition* (Crabb Jr.)
  10
Anderson, Perry 88
Ang Cheng Guan 74
Aristotle 119
Association of Southeast Asian Nations
  (ASEAN) 18, 67, 73, 74, 80

Badawi, Abdullah 68
Bauer, Harry 10
Baumgartner, Frank R. 23
Belt Road Initiative (BRI) *see* One-
  Belt-One-Road (OBOR) initiative
Betts, Richard 104
Big-P pragmatism: agenda-setting
  and 59; continuum of pragmatism
  15, **114**; decision 111; election
  trail 95–100, 105; goals of 39,
  60; in internal/external policy-
  making of state 87; for national
  interest 4, 16; needs of 60; in
  political/institutional contexts
  109; principled pragmatism **114**;
  Small-P and 40, 54–56, 67, 87,
  109–112, 116
Brands, Hal 90
Brighi, Elizabetta 10
Brunei 67
Buddhism 37
Bush, George, Jr. 92, 98–99, 103
Bush, George, Sr. 91, 103

Cambodia–Singapore relations
  72–75
Carter–Deng normalisation 52–55
Chen Yi 46, 50–51
Chiang Kai-shek 41
China 4–5, 20, 28, 67, 109, 112;
  century of humiliation 19; conflicts
  without conflict 39–40; Cultural
  Revolution 117, 118; Five
  Principles of Peaceful Coexistence
  46; foreign policy 12, 49–56;
  government as management
  37–39; Great Leap Forward 118;
  Local People's Congress 43;
  modernisation, Reagan and 97–98;
  One-Belt-One-Road (OBOR)
  initiative 70–71; pragmatism
  in 29–30, 37–42, 55–56, 117;
  relations with Singapore 69–71;

relations with US 71–72, 90–92, 98–99; revolutionaries 40–42; role in Vietnam 91; seeking truth from facts 43–47; US–China Joint Communiqué on Arms Sales to Taiwan (1982) 91, 97; US–China Strategic Economic Dialogue (SED, 2006) 92
China–Singapore Connectivity Initiative (CCI) 70–71
Chinese Communist Party (CCP) 41, 45
Churchill, Winston 90–91
Clinton, Bill 91, 98
Cold War 4, 90, 96, 115
collectivism 41
Communism 41, 43, 69, 104
concept plans 62–63
Confucianism 37, 40
contextualism 17, 115
Coordinated Market Economies 27
'Coping with Vulnerability' (Leifer) 78
cost–benefit analysis 25, 26
Crabb, Cecil V., Jr. 10, 89
Cultural Revolution 44, 117, 118

decision-making 20, 104; international 26; national 25; political 78, 103; pragmatic 63, 66, 111; process 23, 44
defensive realism 22
Deng Xiaoping 40, 43–44, 110, 117, 118; accession to power 38; Carter–Deng normalisation 52–55, 97; and Jiang 39; and Lee Kuan Yew 70; making pragmatism official 46–47; and Mao Zedong 44; reforms 16; statement on pragmatism 1, 43; visited Singapore, in 1978 69
Desker, Barry 74
development guide plans 62–63
Dewey, James 10, 40
Dhanabalan, Suppiah 73
duality 16, 17, 20, 67, 71, 113
Dueck, Colin 89, 90

election trail: Big-P pragmatism on 95–100, 110; Small-P pragmatism on 95–100, 102–103, 110

Engels, F. 37
European Union (EU) 11, 18

Fabian socialism 63
fact-based analysis 11, 24, 51, 61, 116; of evolving situation 26; and inductive analysis of situation 38, 60; of reality 17, 51
Fitzgerald, F. Scott 87
Five Principles of Peaceful Coexistence, China's 46
flexibility in implementation 17, 51, 115
Ford, Gerald 52, 112
Ford, Henry 91
Forum of Small States (FOSS) 63
Four Modernisations Policy 54
Fu Ying 44

Gelb, Leslie 104
Geraldine Chen 78
Ge, Yu 88
Goh Chok Tong 60, 61, 66, 71
Goh Keng Swee 61, 73, 78
Goldstein, Judith 23
Gorbachev, Mikhail 97
government, as management 37–39
grand strategy 4, 17, 113–115
Great Leap Forward 118
Guangzhou Knowledge City project 70

Hall, Peter 27
hierarchy of needs, Maslow's 2
homo economicus model 1
Hong Kong 39, 54, 69
Hon Sui Sen 78
Ho, Peter 62
Houphouët-Boigny, Félix 4
Hua Guofeng 53
Hu Jintao 44, 110
Hun Sen 74
Hunt, Michael 88
Hu Yaobang 53
Hyer, Eric 40
hypocrisy 1, 37

ideology *versus* pragmatism 4, 90
Indonesia 66, 67, 69, 71, 80
inductive situation analysis 38, 60
innenpolitik theories 22

international agenda-setting 26
international formulation 26
international decision-making 26
Iraq 99

James, William 10
Japan 98; Ministry of Trade and
Industry (MITI) 69; wartime
occupation of Singapore 68–69
Jiang Zemin 38, 39, 44, 98
Johnson, Lyndon B. 91
Jones, Bryan D. 23

Kausikan, Bilahari 61, 74
Keohane, Robert O. 23
Khazanah Nasional 68
Kissinger, H. 46, 49, 52, 96, 97
Koh, Tommy 74, 78
Korean People's Army 50
Korean War 96
KTM (Keretapi Tanah Melayu) 68

Lampton, David 44
Laos 73
Lasswell, Harold D. 23
Layne, Christopher 90
Lee Hsien Loong 62, 68, 71, 79, 80
Lee Khoon Choy 67
Lee Kuan Yew 19, 59–63, 67–71,
73, 74, 78, 79
Legalism 37
Leifer, Michael 78
liberalism 4, 9
Liberal Market Economies 27
Lon Nol 74
Low Thia Kiang 80–81

Macau Special Administrative
Regions 54
Macron, Emanuel 5
Mahathir Mohamad 68
Mahbubani, Kishore 82
Malayan Communist Party (MCP)
69
Malaysia 67–69, 71, 73, 80
Mann, James 97
Maoism 45
Mao Zedong 40, 54, 82, 110–111;
On Contradiction 41; and
Deng Xiaoping 43, 44, 53;
ideology 44–45; Nixon–Mao

rapprochement 46, 50–52, 95–96,
112; riding tiger of ideology
44–45
Marx, K. 37
Marxism 41
Maslow's hierarchy of needs 2
master plans 62–63
Mazarin, Cardinal 119
McDougall, Walter A. 88
Mead, Walter Russell 88
Mill, John S. 111
Ministry of Trade and Industry
(MITI), Japan 69
Mintz's poliheuristic model 3–4
Mohist 37

Nathan, S.R. 72–74
national agenda-setting 24
national decision-making 25
national evaluation 26
national formulation 24–25
national implementation 25, 26
Neo Boon Siong 78
neoclassical realism 3, 18, 21, **22**,
23
neopragmatism 9
New START treaty 99
Nixon, R. 46, 91, 116
Nixon–Mao rapprochement 46,
50–52, 95–96, 112, 116
nominalism/priorism 10
non-pragmatism 44, 51, 117;
continuum 4, 14, **15**, **114**;
decisions 13, 24; as directed by
ideology 17, 115; hypothetical
counter-factual scenarios of 28;
pragmatism and 55, 109, 110,
112, 116, 118
North Korea 92
Nye, Joseph 89

Obama, Barack 92, 99
offensive realism **22**
On Contradiction (Mao Zedong) 41
One-Belt-One-Road (OBOR)
initiative 70–71
'one-country-two-systems' approach
39

Paris Peace talks (1989) 74
Peirce, Charles 10

People's Action Party (PAP) 60, 63, 80–82
People's Volunteer Army 50
Philippines 67, 71
philosophical pragmatism 10
phronesis, Aristotelian 119
Pillar, Paul R. 89
policy: cycle approach 18, 23; evaluation 103; formulation 20, 38, 43, 50, 51, 54, 60, 62, 63, 90, 98, 102, 103, 105; implementation 43, 51, 54, 63, 90, 98, 102, 103, 105
policy cycle approach *see* public policy
poliheuristic model, Mintz's 3–4
Popescu, Ionut 90
Pragmatic Dragon (Hyer) 40
pragmatism: as compromise 12–13; definition of 9–13, 110–112; of ends 14–16; geography of 77–83; grand strategy *versus* 4; ideology of/and 4, 59–64, 90, 116–117; in international relations 10, 13, 21–23; of means 14; nature and paradox of 112–115; neopragmatism 9; philosophical 10; pragmatism-as-adaptability 68; principled 115; quasi- 11; in sequence 115–116; survival and 117–118; systemic 119–121; varieties of 27–29, 109–118; *see also* Big-P pragmatism; non-pragmatism; Small-P pragmatism; strategic pragmatism
Pragmatism in Policy Process framework 18, 23–26, 28; context-process models 21–23, **22**; national evaluation 26; national implementation 25, 26; national/ international agenda-setting 24, 26; national/international decision-making 25, 26; national/ international formulation 24–25, 26; policy cycle approach (public policy) 23
Prakash, Chetan 1–2
Preston, Andrew 88
principled pragmatism 115

problem-solving approach 1–6, 11, 18; *see also* pragmatism
public policy 18, 23

quasi-pragmatism 11

Rahim, Lily 69
Rajaratnam, S. 80
Ralston, Shane 10
Ranariddh, Prince 74
Razak, Najib 68
Reagan, Ronald 91, 97–98
realism 92; defensive **22**; liberalism *versus* 4; neoclassical 3, 18, 21, **22**, 23; offensive **22**
realistic analysis 17, 113
Reluctant Crusaders (Dueck) 89
Rorty, Richard 9, 10
Ruihuan, Li 44

Schein, Edgar 61
self-reinforcing belief 82–83
Shanghai Communiqué 51
Sihanouk, Prince 74
Singapore 4, 5, 12, 20, 28, 109; birth-control policy 63–64; Centre for Strategic Futures 62; Economic Development Board (EDB) 61; geography of pragmatism 77–83; konfrontasi era 67–68; learning from Japan 68–69; People's Action Party (PAP) 60, 63, 80–82; poisonous shrimp, ideology of 79; political system 120; pragmatism in 29–30, 59–64, 66–75, 110–111, 117, 118; relations with Cambodia 72–75; relations with China 69–71; unlinking from Malaysia 68; urban planning system 62–63; Urban Redevelopment Authority 62
Singapore–China Suzhou Industrial Park (SIP) 70
Singapore: Identity, Brand, Power (Tan) 77
Small-P pragmatism 14–16, 28, 39, 59, 60; Big-P and 40, 54–56, 67, 87, 109–112, 114; continuum **15**, **114**; election trail 95–100, 104;

for personal interest 4; on policy outcomes 25
Smith, Tony 88
socialism 37
Southern Transport Corridor (STC) 71
South Korea 69
Soviet Union/USSR/Russia 45, 50, 53, 74, 96, 97, 99
Stoessinger, John G. 88
Strategic Arms Limitation Treaty (SALT) 53, 54
strategic pragmatism 4; and China 69–71; continuum 15, 114; and grand strategy 16–17; idea of 112; ingredients of 111; as long-term strategic vision alignment 113; and non-pragmatism 112; systemic and 119–121
structural factors of (pragmatic) production 18–20
Sukarno, President 67
survival, and pragmatism 117–118
systemic pragmatism 119–121

Taiwan 49–51, 53, 54, 69, 92, 97–99
Taiwan Relations Act 97
Tan, Kenneth Paul 77, 116
Taoism 37
Temasek Holdings 68
Thailand 73
Tianjin Eco-City Project (TECP) 70
Trump, Donald 92, 99, 100

United Nations 18, 73, 74
United Nations Transitional Authority of Cambodia (UNTAC) 74
United States (US) 4, 5, 12, 20, 28, 67, 74, 83, 109; 21st-century pragmatism 99–100; Big-P pragmatism on election trail 95–100, 110; check and balance system 103–104; Cold War 4,

90, 96, 115; Congress 95, 97, 98, 100, 103; foreign policy, as product of electoral system 104–105; New START treaty 99; pragmatism in 29–30, 87–92, 110–113; relations with China 71–72, 90–92, 98–99; Small-P pragmatism on election trail 95–100, 102–103, 110; State Department 103; Taiwan Relations Act 97; US–China Joint Communiqué on Arms Sales to Taiwan (1982) 91, 97; US–China Relations Act of 2000 91; US–China Strategic Economic Dialogue (SED, 2006) 92
unpragmatism 11, 27, 29
urban planners 62–63

Varieties of Capitalism (Hall) 27
Vietnam: China's role in 91; invasion of Cambodia 73, 80
Vietnam War 95, 104

Walt, Stephen 89, 90
Wang Huning 39
War on Terror 98–99
Watergate scandal 52
What Good is Grand Strategy? (Brands) 90
Wilson, Woodrow 43
wish-based analysis 17, 24, 103, 115
Wolfowitz, Paul 99
World Trade Organisation 38

Xi Jinping 38–39, 44, 47

Yeo, Philip 62
Yu Huaiyan 89

Zakaria, Fareed 104
Zhang Baijia 40
Zhao Qizheng 44
Zhou Enlai 40, 45–46, 52
Zhu Rongji 44